GRADE
6

STAAR Reading
PRACTICE

Table of Contents

Using This Book

What Is the STAAR Reading Assessment?

The State of Texas Assessments of Academic Readiness (STAAR) is the current assessment for students in the state of Texas. STAAR Reading assesses what students are expected to learn at each grade level according to the developmentally appropriate academic readiness and supporting standards outlined in the Texas Essential Knowledge and Skills (TEKS).

How Does This Book Help My Student(s)?

If your student is taking the STAAR Assessment for Reading, then as a teacher and/or parent you can use the practice passages and text-dependent questions in this book to prepare for the STAAR Reading exam. This book is appropriate for on-grade-level students.

STAAR Reading Practice provides:

- Leveled practice with assessed genres
- Text-dependent comprehension and vocabulary questions
- Questions in short-answer and multiple-choice format
- Opportunities to familiarize students with STAAR format and question stems

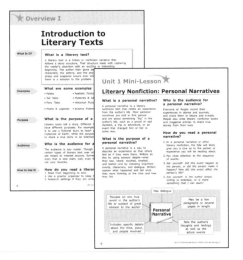

Introduce text type and genres

Practice reading passages

Assess comprehension and vocabulary with text-dependent comprehension questions

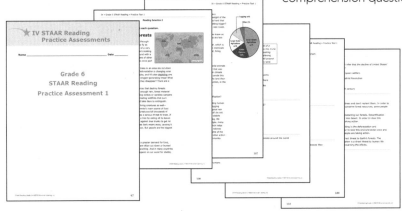

Simulate test-taking with full-length practice tests

What Does STAAR Reading Assess?

The STAAR Grade 6 Reading Assessment assesses the following:

Genres Assessed:	Literary	Informational
	• Fiction (Readiness)	• Expository (Readiness)
	• Literary Nonfiction (Supporting)	• Persuasive (Supporting)
	• Poetry (Supporting)	• Procedural (Embedded)
	• Drama (Supporting)	• Media Literacy (Embedded)
	• Media Literacy (Embedded)	

Reporting Category 1: Understanding Across Genres
Demonstrate an ability to understand a variety of written texts across reading genres.

(2) Understand new vocabulary and use it when reading and writing.

(3) Analyze, make inferences, and draw conclusions about theme and genre in different cultural, historical, and contemporary contexts and provide evidence from the text to support their understanding.

(7) Understand, make inferences, and draw conclusions about the varied structural patterns and features of literary nonfiction and provide evidence from text to support their understanding.

(9) Analyze, make inferences, and draw conclusions about the author's purpose in cultural, historical, and contemporary contexts and provide evidence from the text to support their understanding.

(11) Analyze, make inferences, and draw conclusions about persuasive text and provide evidence from text to support their analysis.

(Fig. 19) Use a flexible range of metacognitive reading skills in both assigned and independent reading to understand an author's message. Students will continue to apply earlier standards with greater depth in increasingly more complex texts as they become self-directed, critical readers.

Reporting Category 2: Understanding and Analysis of Literary Texts
Demonstrate an ability to understand and analyze literary texts.

(3) Analyze, make inferences, and draw conclusions about theme and genre in different cultural, historical, and contemporary contexts and provide evidence from the text to support their understanding.

(4) Understand, make inferences, and draw conclusions about the structure and elements of poetry and provide evidence from the text to support their understanding.

(5) Understand, make inferences, and draw conclusions about the structure and elements of drama and provide evidence from the text to support their understanding.

(6) Understand, make inferences, and draw conclusions about the structure and elements of fiction and provide evidence from text to support their understanding.

(8) Understand, make inferences, and draw conclusions about how an author's sensory language creates imagery in literary text and provide evidence from text to support their understanding.

(13) Use comprehension skills to analyze how words, images, graphics, and sounds work together in various forms to impact meaning. Students will continue to apply earlier standards with greater depth in increasingly more complex texts.

(Fig. 19) Use a flexible range of metacognitive reading skills in both assigned and independent reading to understand an author's message and will continue to apply earlier standards with greater depth in increasingly more complex texts as they become self-directed, critical readers.

Reporting Category 3: Understanding and Analysis of Informational Texts Demonstrate an ability to understand and analyze informational texts.

(10) Analyze, make inferences, and draw conclusions about expository text and provide evidence from text to support their understanding.

(11) Analyze, make inferences, and draw conclusions about persuasive text and provide evidence from text to support their analysis.

(12) Understand how to glean and use information in procedural texts and documents.

(13) Use comprehension skills to analyze how words, images, graphics, and sounds work together in various forms to impact meaning. Students will continue to apply earlier standards with greater depth in increasingly more complex texts.

(Fig. 19) Use a flexible range of metacognitive reading skills in both assigned and independent reading to understand an author's message. Students will continue to apply earlier standards with greater depth in increasingly more complex texts as they become self-directed, critical readers.

Introduction to Literary Texts

What Is It?

What is a literary text?

A literary text is a fiction or nonfiction narrative that follows a story structure. That structure leads by capturing the reader's attention with an exciting or interesting beginning. The author then gives details about the characters, the setting, and the plot. Usually a problem arises and suspense occurs over what will happen. Finally, there is a solution to the problem.

Examples

What are some examples of a literary text?

- Fables
- Tall Tales
- Fairy Tales
- Myths & Legends
- Poetry
- Realistic Fiction
- Mysteries & Adventure
- Historical Fiction
- Science Fiction
- Drama & Plays
- Literary Nonfiction
- Biographies
- Journals & Diaries
- Personal Narratives
- Memoirs

Purpose

What is the purpose of a literary text?

Literary texts tell a story. Different types of narratives will have different purposes. For example, the purpose of a fable is to use a fictional story to teach people lessons or explain mysteries of Earth, while the purpose of literary nonfiction is to share a true story in an interesting or entertaining way.

Audience

Who is the audience for a literary text?

The audience is any reader. Though many people prefer certain types of literary text over other types, the stories are meant to interest anyone. Sometimes you will enjoy a story that is told really well, even though the story line is not your favorite.

How to Use It

How do you read a literary text?

1. Read from beginning to end.
2. Use a graphic organizer to keep the characters straight.
3. Research settings if they are unfamiliar.

What are some common features of a literary text?

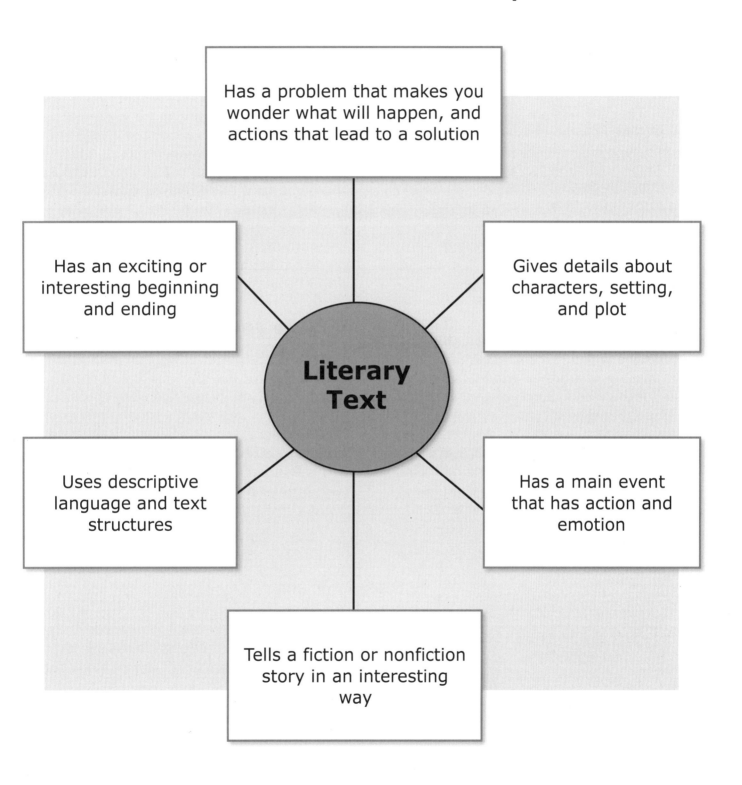

Has a problem that makes you wonder what will happen, and actions that lead to a solution

Has an exciting or interesting beginning and ending

Gives details about characters, setting, and plot

Literary Text

Uses descriptive language and text structures

Has a main event that has action and emotion

Tells a fiction or nonfiction story in an interesting way

Literary Nonfiction: Memoirs

What is a memoir?

A memoir is an autobiographical nonfiction text that retells an experience from the author's life. Most memoirs cover a short period of time in the author's life. Memoirs focus on the events, thoughts, and feelings of that person. They are often about a specific time or place or a moment in history that is important to the writer. Memoirs communicate the conflict and drama of events with a strong, personal point of view.

What is the purpose of a memoir?

The purpose of a memoir is to describe events as the writer remembers them. These writers want to share their experiences with the rest of the world. Some writers may have lived through important times or contributed to world-changing events. They want readers to know what they did and to share what they felt. Writers may also use the memoir as a journey of self-discovery. Writing about the past can help people better understand themselves and how they came to be who they are.

Who is the audience for a memoir?

Everyone is! In the past, people who took part in world-changing events, like explorations or scientific discoveries, wrote memoirs. The writers wanted to give an eyewitness account of the event. But today, you don't have to be famous to write a memoir. Memoirs can be about everyday events as well as world-changing moments. They are often appealing to readers because of the funny, dramatic, or touching way the writer remembers and explains the events.

How do you read a memoir?

A memoir is a personal narrative so as a reader, you must enter into the moment with the writer. Try to picture yourself there. Think about what is important and why the writer chose to write about the event. Pay attention to the description and look for insight into why the writer remembered the moment in such great detail.

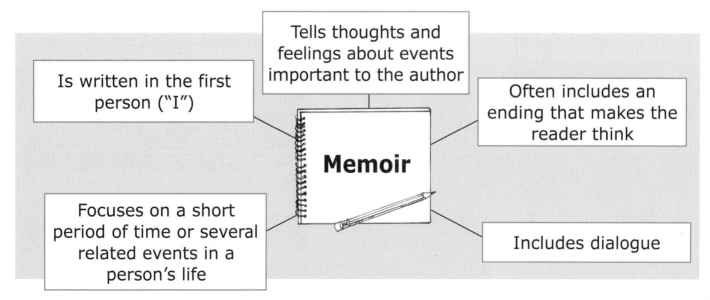

- Is written in the first person ("I")
- Tells thoughts and feelings about events important to the author
- Often includes an ending that makes the reader think
- Focuses on a short period of time or several related events in a person's life
- **Memoir**
- Includes dialogue

Read the selection. Then choose the best answer to each question.

We Shall Not Be Moved

1   My Grandpa David is my role model. He is the reason I marched for civil rights, why I think <u>discrimination</u> and prejudice are wrong, and why I've made friends with people from different cultures.

2   When I was born in 1944, Grandpa David Greenspan was living with my mother and father in the Bronx. The Bronx is a part of New York City. He had left his Polish homeland as a young man in 1910 because he did not want to fight in the army. Grandpa believed in peace, not war.

3   Grandpa was a very accepting and open-minded person. Once, he came home to our little apartment on Bolton Street with a homeless man. From then on, this man would come over every Tuesday night for dinner. It was through my Grandpa's actions, his kindness to others, and his uncompromising humanity that I learned the right way to treat people.

4   One of my closest friends in school was Stokely Carmichael, a future leader of an activist organization. We were in high school in the late 1950s. At that time, the civil rights movement was sweeping across America. A few years earlier, the Supreme Court had declared that separating people on the basis of race was illegal. But segregation and inequality still existed in many places. Stokely began participating in demonstrations around New York City. A demonstration is a rally for people who support a cause. He joined the Freedom Riders. I joined the National Conference of Christians and Jews. That is an organization dedicated to promoting peace and tolerance in a world of diversity.

5   Despite what the law said, many businesses still discriminated. They would not offer jobs to people of other races. Early one Saturday morning when I was thirteen, I went to picket, or protest, at Macy's because the store wouldn't hire African Americans. A crowd of people from different backgrounds carried picket signs that said "Jobs Now!" and "Full Employment!" We marched and sang protest songs like "We Shall Not Be Moved."

6   Music was an important part of the civil rights movement. Singer-songwriters such as Pete Seeger, Joan Baez, and Bob Dylan drew heavily from traditional folk music and popularized protest songs. In 1964, President Lyndon Johnson passed the Civil Rights Act. This was an executive order making it illegal to discriminate against anyone on the basis of race, color, religion, sex, or national origin.

7   The sum of a person is more than her parts. If I were an equation, it might look like this: Grandpa David + Civil Rights + Music = Me.

Name _____ **Date** _____

1   The word <u>discrimination</u> in paragraph 1 means —

_____

_____

_____

_____

2   Where does this story take place?

_____

_____

_____

_____

3   What detail in this story shows the reader that Grandpa was an accepting and open-minded person?

_____

_____

_____

_____

4   Give an example of a civil right.

_____

_____

_____

_____

Name _____ **Date** _____

5 What year was the writer born?

  A 1950

  B 1964

  C 1944

  D 1910

6 Why did Grandpa David leave Poland in 1910?

  A He was against discrimination and prejudice.

  B He liked New York.

  C He wanted to be with his family.

  D He didn't want to fight in the army.

7 Businesses were breaking the law in the 1950s by —

  A participating in demonstrations

  B participating in the civil rights movement

  C not offering jobs to people of all races

  D picketing

8 The reader can conclude that President Lyndon Johnson —

  A supported civil rights

  B fought against civil rights

  C was in office in the 1940s

  D was friends with Grandpa David

Read the selection. Then choose the best answer to each question.

A New Beginning

1   In the years before I started high school, I wasn't very good at . . . well, anything. For instance, I wasn't any good at playing baseball—when my friends chose up sides for a ball game, I was always the last one to get picked.

2   I wasn't any good at hide-and-seek. When I closed my eyes to count to one hundred, I think my friends just went home.

3   Playing tag wasn't any better for me, either. When I was tagged and was "it," I stayed "it," and as far as I know, I'm still "it."

4   When I got a little older and it came to girls, forget about it—I figured I was as interesting to girls as a fire hydrant. Across the hall from our apartment lived Mary. Mary was the prettiest girl in the world. The problem was that Mary dated older boys who slicked their hair back and wore black leather jackets, a look I could never pull off.

5   The only thing I was any good at was reading. I liked to read books, such as Ian Fleming's James Bond novels, techno thrillers, science fiction, the Hardy Boys books, and Sherlock Holmes detective stories.

6   In September 1963, everything changed for me. I started high school. I wanted to go to the nearby high school with the neighborhood kids, but my English teacher, Sister Elizabeth, had other ideas. She wanted me to attend Cardinal Spellman High School, a scholarship high school only kids with good grades could attend.

7   "At Spellman you'll get a better education," Sister Elizabeth said, "and you'll be better prepared for college." My future was cast!

8   When I started going to classes at Spellman, I met lots of kids like me—boys and girls who were smart and good at reading; nobody cared that I stank at baseball, hide-and-seek, and tag.

9   I joined the Spellman marching band and learned to play the clarinet. Every day after school we had band practice. And at practice, I couldn't keep my eyes off a pretty blonde freshman named Cathy who sat nearby and played the saxophone. When I looked at her, she actually smiled at me.

10   One afternoon after practice, Cathy and I happened to walk out of the band room at the same time.

11   "The school dance is this Friday night," she said to me. "Wanna go to the dance with me?"

12   In my astonished state, all I could say was a <u>meek</u> "okay." Cathy wrote her address on a slip of paper and gave it to me. I looked at the address and noticed her street wasn't far from school.

13   "Can I walk you home?" I asked with my heart pounding.

Name _____ **Date** _____

1 Where does the writer go to high school?

_____

_____

_____

_____

2 What details from the selection show what the writer was like before
   high school?

_____

_____

_____

_____

3 How does life change for the writer when he starts at Spellman?

_____

_____

_____

_____

4 What clue shows that the writer is nervous about asking Cathy to
   walk home?

_____

_____

_____

_____

Name _____ **Date** _____

5 The word <u>meek</u> means —

   A loud

   B shy

   C excited

   D terrified

---

6 Sister Elizabeth suggests the writer go to Spellman because —

   A his friends are going there

   B the school has a good baseball team

   C he can get a better education there

   D she teaches there

---

7 Which detail shows that Cathy likes the writer?

   A She plays the saxophone.

   B She has blonde hair.

   C She goes to Spellman, too.

   D She asks him to the dance.

---

8 Which of the following will happen next?

   A Cathy will smile at the writer.

   B Sister Elizabeth will suggest the writer go to Spellman.

   C The writer will walk Cathy home.

   D The writer and Cathy will go to the dance.

Unit 2 Mini-Lesson ★
Historical Fiction

What is historical fiction?

Historical fiction stories take place in the past. Historical fiction stories have characters, settings, and events based on historical facts. The characters can be based on real people or made up. The dialogue is made up. But the information about the time period must be authentic, or factually accurate.

What is the purpose of historical fiction?

Historical fiction blends history and fiction into stories that could have actually happened. It adds a human element to history. Readers can learn about the time period: how people lived, what they owned, and even what they ate and wore. Readers can also see how people's problems and feelings have not changed much over time.

Who tells the story in historical fiction?

Authors often write historical fiction from the first person point of view, wherein one character tells the story as it happens to him or her (using words such as **I** and **our**). In the third person point of view, a narrator tells the story and refers to the characters using words such as **he** and **her**, or by name.

How do you read historical fiction?

1. Look to the title for clues about an important time, place, character, or situation.
2. Note how the characters' lives compare to yours.
3. Note the main characters' thoughts, feelings, and actions, and how they change during the story.
4. Consider what you can learn today from people's struggles long ago.

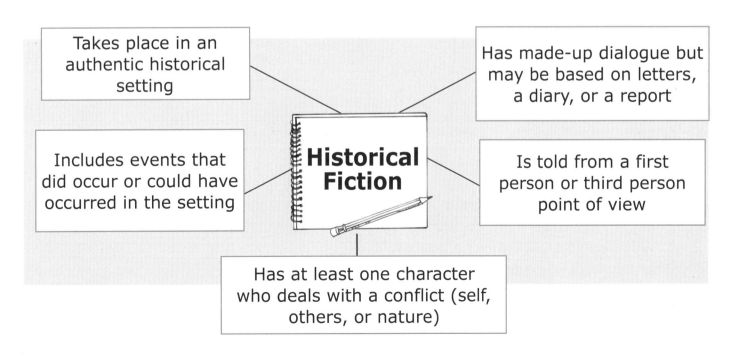

Takes place in an authentic historical setting

Has made-up dialogue but may be based on letters, a diary, or a report

Includes events that did occur or could have occurred in the setting

Historical Fiction

Is told from a first person or third person point of view

Has at least one character who deals with a conflict (self, others, or nature)

Read the selection. Then choose the best answer to each question.

The Strong and the Weak: Hammurabi's Code

1   Ditanu was carving a plaque, following a pattern his master had created. His master was Belshunu, a stone carver. Ditanu had been living in the home of his uncle Lamusa, a violent man. But Belshunu had offered Ditanu an apprenticeship, as well as a home. Lamusa was happy that he did not have to worry about the boy any longer.

2   This morning Ditanu was perfectly happy. The future looked very bright.

3   A well-dressed woman stormed into the shop. "I am the Wife of Hudu-libbi," said the woman. "I want you to make a votive figure of me," she told Belshunu.

4   Only priests could go into the hearts of temples where gods were worshipped. So wealthy people commissioned statues called votives so they were able to pray constantly to the gods.

5   "I'm afraid I'm busy with a royal commission. It's inscribed with King Hammurabi's laws. My apprentice Ditanu will make your votive."

6   The Wife of Hudu-libbi looked over at the young man and said, "I'm going to stay and make sure this boy doesn't try to cheat me."

7   Ditanu rushed to finish the statue. He carefully reduced the size of the votive's nose. Then he engraved lines and zigzags representing the Wife of Hudu-libbi's jewelry. When he finished, the woman came over and scrutinized the votive figure.

8   "It looks almost entirely like me!" Before he could thank her, Ditanu heard a voice from the courtyard that sent a shiver up his spine.

9   His disheveled uncle headed straight to Belshunu. "I've come to take my nephew off your hands," Lamusa said. "Come, dear nephew, and bring that pouch of silver with you."

10   "The boy stays here."

11   Everyone looked around. "Says who? Some nameless woman?"

12   "Law eighty-eight: 'If an artisan has undertaken to rear a child and teaches him his craft, the child cannot be demanded back.'" The Wife of Hudu-libbi continued in thunderous tones, "You would break Hammurabi's laws and welcome the wrath of the gods?"

13   Shamash, who sat upright on a throne, looked especially intimidating. Lamusa turned pale under the gaze of the god. "I suppose you can keep the boy," he told Belshunu.

14   Lamusa turned and skulked off. Thanks to the Wife of Hudu-libbi, Ditanu now knew that his home and bright future were both carved in stone.

Name _____ **Date** _____

1 The word <u>apprenticeship</u> in paragraph 1 means —

_____

_____

_____

_____

2 What is Ditanu training to be?

_____

_____

_____

_____

3 Which detail shows that the Wife of Hudu-libbi was suspicious of Ditanu at first?

_____

_____

_____

_____

4 The reader can conclude that Ditanu's future is bright because —

_____

_____

_____

_____

Name _____ **Date** _____

5 Who is Belshunu's apprentice?

A Ditanu

B Lamusa

C Hudu-libbi

D King Hammurabi

6 Lamusa most likely wants his nephew back because he —

A misses Ditanu

B wants Ditanu's money

C wants Ditanu to carve a votive figure for him

D wants Ditanu to be his apprentice

7 Who says, "The boy stays here"?

A Shamash

B Belshunu

C Lamusa

D the Wife of Hudu-libbi

8 Why does Lamusa most likely decide Belshunu can keep Ditanu?

A fear

B boredom

C anger

D money

Read the selection. Then choose the best answer to each question.

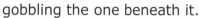

The Day the Towers Fell

1   "Ninety-nine point six degrees," Mom said, reading the thermometer she'd just pulled out of my mouth. "Your fever is down but not completely gone."

2   She'd missed work yesterday to stay with me; she couldn't afford to miss another day and had to leave almost immediately so she wouldn't be late. She always took the subway from our apartment in Chelsea to her receptionist job in the financial district of New York City.

3   Today was September 11, 2001, and it started out as a gloriously sunny day to stay home from school. I found the remote, flopped onto the sofa, and turned on the television. There was some movie on about a burning skyscraper, but as I watched, it began to look more like one of those special news programs that interrupt a regularly scheduled show. I tried channel after channel, but the same program was being broadcast on each one.

4   They were talking about the World Trade Center, which was where my mom worked. "Two commercial airliners have flown into the Twin Towers," the newscaster was saying. I ran to my bedroom and looked out the window. It was real, all right, and Mom's office was on the thirty-first floor of the North Tower.

5   Outside, the uppermost part of the South Tower—the part above the burning <u>gash</u>—tilted slightly, drooping toward the ground. Then it dropped. In one long and devastating moment, the building collapsed downward, each floor gobbling the one beneath it.

6   I raced to the ringing telephone in the kitchen and pounced on it. "Mom? Hello? Mom?"

7   "Aaron?" It was Mom. I collapsed onto the linoleum floor with relief.

8   "Are you all right?" she asked.

9   "I'm fine," I replied. "Are you all right? Where are you?"

10   "I'm in the lobby of a bank," Mom answered. "I'm okay. I'm on my way home."

11   As I watched the North Tower fall, I learned that there had been four concurrent hijackings—a third airplane had crashed into the Pentagon and a fourth went down in a field in Pennsylvania. When my mom finally made it home, she was exhausted, bedraggled, and covered in white dust. Her hands and knees were bandaged. She cried as I hugged her.

12   "I . . . I . . . I was two blocks away from my office when the North Tower was hit," she stuttered. "I heard a terrible roar, and everyone around me started screaming and running. I looked back to see a tidal wave of ash and dust and debris coming down the street. In the panic I tripped and fell, but I managed to get up and duck into the nearest doorway just as the debris cloud hit."

Name _____ **Date** _____

1 The word <u>gash</u> in paragraph 5 means —

_____

_____

_____

_____

2 How can the reader tell Aaron has been sick?

_____

_____

_____

_____

3 What does Aaron see when he looks out his bedroom window?

_____

_____

_____

_____

4 Why does Aaron's mother cry when he hugs her?

_____

_____

_____

_____

Name _____ **Date** _____

5 Where does Aaron's mother work?

    A in Chelsea

    B in the North Tower of the World Trade Center

    C in the South Tower of the World Trade Center

    D at a bank

6 Read this passage from paragraph 5.

> . . . the building collapsed downward, each floor gobbling the one beneath it.

The imagery in this passage engages the reader's sense of —

    A smell

    B touch

    C taste

    D sight

7 Why does Aaron collapse in the kitchen?

    A He doesn't feel well.

    B He trips.

    C He's relieved that his mother is okay.

    D He's upset, fearing that his mother is in the North Tower.

8 Which happens first to Aaron's mom?

    A Aaron hugs her.

    B She hears a terrible roar.

    C She ducks into a doorway.

    D She trips and falls.

Myths and Legends

What are myths and legends?

A myth is a traditional story from an ancient culture that explains natural occurrences, such as how the world began or why the world is the way it is. The main character is often a god, goddess, or hero with special powers. A legend is a story based on a famous figure, place, or event. Legends are usually based on historical events, but they are fictionalized.

What is the purpose of myths and legends?

Long ago, people relied on myths and legends to explain natural events, such as violent storms or how a mountain came to be. Myths and legends were used to educate and entertain as part of a tradition of oral, or spoken, storytelling. Both legends and myths tell inspiring or cautionary adventure stories about people, places, or events that were important to a culture. Listeners learn good values from the actions of the heroes who are strong, brave, and honest.

Who is the audience for myths and legends?

In ancient times, storytellers told myths and legends to answer questions about the world and to pass on their culture from one generation to the next. As the centuries passed, these stories were told and retold and then written down. Today science has explained the events in myths, but readers still enjoy the exciting adventures.

How do you read myths and legends?

As you read a myth, think about how the event is explained. Ask yourself: *What does the main character do? How do these actions help explain an event?* Do not look for a factual retelling of events or realistic portrayals of characters when you read a legend. Instead, look for unusual details and extraordinary people or creatures. Ask yourself what parts of the legend might be true and what parts make the legend unbelievable.

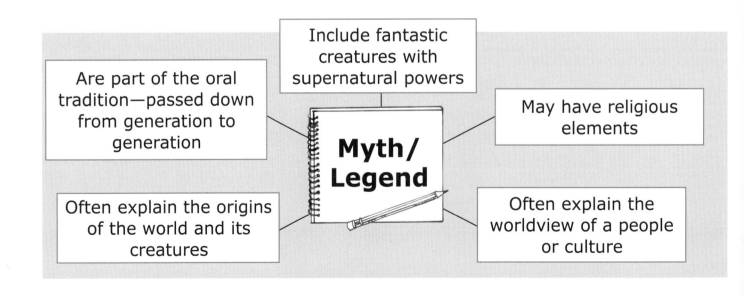

Are part of the oral tradition—passed down from generation to generation

Include fantastic creatures with supernatural powers

May have religious elements

Myth/ Legend

Often explain the origins of the world and its creatures

Often explain the worldview of a people or culture

Read the selection. Then choose the best answer to each question.

Ra Creates the World

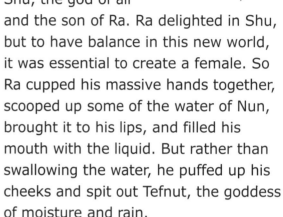

1   Close your eyes and notice the nothingness. That is all that existed before Ra created the world. Unlike other nothingness, however, this one had a name—Nun.

2   The nothingness named Nun groaned under its own weight, but inside Nun's heaviness was a force willing itself into being—a force named Ra. Ra burst through the black sea and his piercing voice shattered the quietude. He pushed and pushed until he had created a large mound. "I am Ra, the Shining One!" shouted the newly emerged force as he stood on top of the mound. He was glistening brightly, for he radiated light; and where the nothingness was once dark, the light of Ra now shone upon it.

3   Ra looked around with his one giant eye, displeased that there was only the solitary mound. "I will create a great city!" he declared. So Ra created a magnificent city on top of the mound. The city was indeed beautiful, but it was devoid of creatures or other living things. So Ra created every animal and all vegetation on Earth and named them. "Here are fat cattle, and here are mighty oaks, and here are tiny frogs," said Ra. He went on and on, designating all he had created. Ra was pleased, though he felt something was still missing.

4   "I must have children," he exclaimed. "Children who will bring me joy in my youth and care for me in my old age." Ra's desire for children was so great that just as he had willed himself into being, he brought up a giant sneeze from his soul.

5   "Shu!" cried out Ra as he sneezed, and so appeared Shu, the god of air and the son of Ra. Ra delighted in Shu, but to have balance in this new world, it was essential to create a female. So Ra cupped his massive hands together, scooped up some of the water of Nun, brought it to his lips, and filled his mouth with the liquid. But rather than swallowing the water, he puffed up his cheeks and spit out Tefnut, the goddess of moisture and rain.

6   Ra was extremely satisfied with all he had created. His greatest satisfaction, however, was found in being a father to Shu and Tefnut. One fateful day, Shu and Tefnut wandered off to play in the dark sea of Nun. When they were gone for what Ra thought was an extraordinary amount of time, he became quite concerned. Ra had a removable eye that he could detach from his face, so he sent his eye to go look for his lost children. In the place of that eye, another appeared.

7   After Ra had waited anxiously for some time, his first eye returned with the lost children. The first eye saw the second eye on Ra's face and became fiercely jealous. Ra took the jealous first eye and placed it on his forehead, where it sat forever as a special watcher over the world.

8   Ra's joy at having his children back was immeasurable. He was so elated that happy tears fell from his eyes—and that is how he created our ancestors.

Name _____ **Date** _____

1 What does the word <u>quietude</u> mean in paragraph 2?

_____

_____

_____

_____

2 How do Nun and Ra differ?

_____

_____

_____

_____

3 What reason does Ra give for bringing children into the world?

_____

_____

_____

_____

4 Why was Ra's first eye jealous?

_____

_____

_____

_____

Name _____ **Date** _____

5 According to the storyteller, who created the world?

 A Nun

 B Shu

 C Ra

 D Tefnut

6 What did Ra create right after he created the city?

 A animals and vegetation

 B children

 C a mound

 D light

7 Who is Tefnut?

 A Ra's son

 B Ra's first eye

 C the god of air

 D Ra's daughter

8 The main purpose of this myth is to —

 A tell how the gods came to be

 B explain the origins of the world and its creatures

 C explain how we came to have two eyes

 D describe how sheep and frogs came to be

Read the selection. Then choose the best answer to each question.

Atlantis: Land of Sunken Dreams

1   Thousands of years ago, the mighty Greek god Poseidon ruled the sea, storms, and earthquakes. Poseidon was enamored of, or in love with, a human woman named Cleito. He was so enthralled, or charmed, by Cleito that he married her. Then he whisked her off to one of his islands. He then had a <u>lavish</u>, or fancy, mountaintop palace built especially for Cleito. Poseidon created an entire nation for Cleito. The humans that inhabited, or lived on, the island were intelligent and compassionate, or kind. These were the type of people he wanted to surround and protect his bride.

2   Poseidon and Cleito had many children. Atlas was their oldest son. He became the island nation's ruler, and so it came to be called the "island of Atlas," or, in Greek, "Atlantis."

3   The people of Atlantis respected one another. They treated one another with kindness. There were no fights, crimes, or arguments of any kind.

4   "Perhaps we need a law saying Atlanteans should devote, or set aside, one day a week for sorrow and suffering," joked Atlas one day. "Perhaps our people will then appreciate our perfect existence."

5   "We don't have sorrow and suffering here," said the citizens of Atlantis. "That's because we are better, smarter, more honest, and more productive than everyone else!" Atlas exclaimed, with a hearty laugh. "It's true—we are above others."

6   That very day, the Atlanteans, feeling a little too smug, or proud, decided it was their moral obligation, or duty, to go out and tell other nations of their superiority.

7   So the Atlanteans set out to tell the rest of the world the news of their greatness. But to the great surprise of the Atlanteans, they were not welcomed for bringing their knowledge of paradise and perfection. Instead, they were treated as hostile invaders, or enemies. So the Atlanteans fought and conquered each nation they came across.

8   Atlas was outraged, or very angry, at what had become of his people and his peaceful island nation. So he thought of a solution. As the Atlanteans prepared for another battle, an explosion more powerful than any on Earth before or since rocked the island nation. The crust of Earth cracked open at the center of the island. Clouds of ash and steam darkened the skies. The island began to disappear into the hole in Earth.

9   In just one day, the entire empire of Atlantis, with all its wealth and power, all its knowledge and artistry, all its history and ambition, disappeared into the sea. Atlantis was sunk by its own selfishness.

Name _____ **Date** _____

1 Poseidon is the ruler of —

_____

_____

_____

_____

2 What evidence from the story shows that Poseidon cared greatly for Cleito?

_____

_____

_____

_____

3 Why did the Atlanteans believe they were "above others"?

_____

_____

_____

_____

4 Why did the rest of the world react to the Atlanteans with hostility?

_____

_____

_____

_____

Name _____ **Date** _____

5 The word <u>lavish</u> means —

   A in love

   B charmed

   C luxurious

   D kind

6 Who was the island nation's ruler?

   A Atlas

   B Poseidon

   C Cleito

   D Atlantis

7 What happened just before Earth cracked open?

   A The Atlanteans told the world of their greatness.

   B Clouds of ash and steam darkened the sky.

   C Atlantis disappeared into Earth.

   D There was an explosion.

8 Atlantis sank into the sea because its citizens had become too —

   A wealthy

   B selfish

   C knowledgeable

   D powerful

Unit 4 Mini-Lesson ★
Science Fiction

What is science fiction?

Science fiction stories use scientific facts and technological developments to imagine a world that doesn't yet exist—but could. Sometimes the science is based on facts, and sometimes it is based on speculation. Often, the science and technology lead to a problem. Science fiction stories often take place in unusual settings, including outer space or distant futures.

What is the purpose of science fiction?

The purpose of science fiction is to reflect on how we live today by exploring imagined worlds. It sets out a possible (though sometimes highly improbable) situation and then explores it, usually in a serious way. Science fiction hopes to make readers think about the consequences today's actions may have for the future.

Who invented science fiction?

Some say that science fiction was invented when someone imagined an alternate world or life on another planet. In the early 1700s, Jonathan Swift wrote about a world with only tiny beings. In the early 1800s, Mary Shelley wrote about a scientist who brings a monster to life using body parts of dead people. More recent writers have explored the effect of computers and artificial intelligence on human beings and the universe.

How do you read science fiction?

Look for science and technology when you read science fiction. Ask yourself how these things are altering or changing the characters. Keep an open mind as you read. You are entering into a world of "what if." It might be a world of the future or the past. It might be on another planet or in another universe. It might even be a frightening world. But it is going to be an interesting trip.

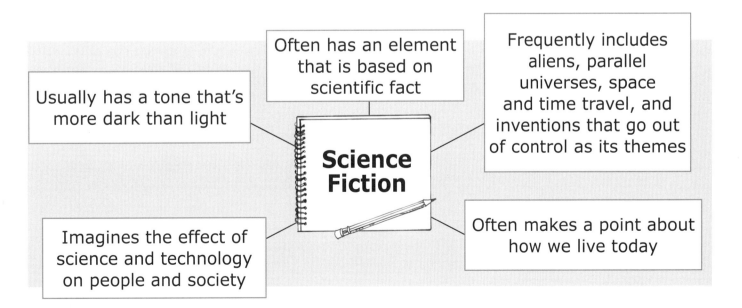

Usually has a tone that's more dark than light

Often has an element that is based on scientific fact

Frequently includes aliens, parallel universes, space and time travel, and inventions that go out of control as its themes

Imagines the effect of science and technology on people and society

Science Fiction

Often makes a point about how we live today

Read the selection. Then choose the best answer to each question.

Dream Pilot

1   Out in space, dreams are very, very bad. I'm a pilot and am trained in everything from engine repair to navigation. But the biggest problem I face during star travel is loneliness. Starships travel very fast—faster even than the speed of light. The human brain isn't wired to handle that kind of speed, and it drives most people crazy.

2   I'm different. When I was a cadet in the Interstellar Exploratory Fleet, doctors determined that with rigorous training my brain could handle the nightmares of deep space. So I became a pilot because a pilot never, ever sleeps.

3   Nearing the halfway point between Earth and the faraway star of Tau Ceti, things are on schedule and going A-OK. Then, turning down the corridor, I spot a lurking monster—an enormous beast, bristling with spiky tufts of fur. It has nothing that looks like a head—instead, a cluster of serpentine tentacles grows from its neck. The monster makes a sound like pudding being sucked from a boot.

4   I calmly approach the monster and walk past it. I don't give it a second glance because I know it will fade away—as long as I pay no attention to it.

5   In the galley, I open the cabinet where the food processors are kept. Inside, a creature with long claws hangs upside down, its grapefruit-sized red eyes glaring at me. Through its translucent skin, I can see branching blood vessels. I ignore this creature, too, and check the temperature meters on the processors.

6   The monsters with their bulging eyes, long tentacles, and razor-edged teeth are all just parts of my waking nightmares. When ships go faster than the speed of light, space gets twisted and warped around them. The brain reacts with hideous nightmares.

7   I'm about to check on the water recyclers when the ship's alarm bells start screaming. I rush to the cockpit and activate the ship's sensors.

8   A four-engined ship looms in my view screen, but its design is nothing like an Earth vessel. It is an alien ship.

9   A moment later, an incoming transmission arrives from the alien ship, and a scream freezes in my throat. The creature on my view screen has no head. Instead, tentacles extend from its neck; on the end of each tentacle a mouth with sharp teeth repeatedly snaps open and shut.

10   I know this monster—I saw it only a few minutes ago. It's the creature from the corridor, the one I ignored. The one I believed was only a nightmare. And it's not alone—next to it is the very same creature I saw in the food processor cabinet.

11   Are my nightmares dreams or are they really real? Or have I lost my mind to the empty reaches of deep space? I have to consider the possibility that I've gone mad. So I do the only sane thing I can think of—I arm the ship's missiles and place my hand on the launch button . . .

Name _____ **Date** _____

1 What is the narrator's job?

_____

_____

_____

_____

2 The word <u>translucent</u> in paragraph 5 means —

_____

_____

_____

_____

3 At first the narrator doesn't think the monsters are real because —

_____

_____

_____

_____

4 Where does this story take place?

_____

_____

_____

_____

Name _____ **Date** _____

5 What is the narrator's biggest problem?

 A engine repair

 B loneliness

 C bad dreams

 D navigation

6 Read this sentence from the selection.

> *The monster makes a sound like pudding being sucked from a boot.*

The imagery in this engages the reader's sense of —

 A smell

 B sight

 C hearing

 D taste

7 Why does the narrator ignore the monsters?

 A to make them go away

 B to annoy them

 C to show them he's not afraid of them

 D to scare them

8 You can tell the narrator ultimately believes the monsters are real because —

 A he screams

 B the monsters touch him

 C the monsters are different from the ones in his dreams

 D he arms the ship's missiles

Read the selection. Then choose the best answer to each question.

Varuna Takes a Job with the Census

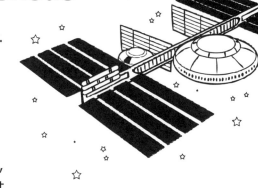

1   Varuna is moments away from being transported to UC, Universe Central. There she is going to take her first job, working for the Universal Census: a count of all sentient beings in the universe that happens once every ten billion years. Varuna, being a Plynchin, has a few advantages for this job. She carries her own ecosystem. A Plynchin is a self-contained unit with extra-dimensional defenses against any outside forces that might disrupt her breathing, nourishment, and so on.

2   Varuna gets a view of the capital city of Universe Central as she beams in. It is spectacular. Its hubs and spokes and spires and wings stretch across the distance among a thousand stars, and in fact hundreds of stars are captured within force fields.

3   Then Varuna finds herself in a smelly methane swamp, the office of Gphimpy, her new boss. Gphimpy explains to Varuna that her job is to find every sentient being in Sector 689,142.021A-&.5. "Last time that was about eighty billion beings, so you'd better get cracking!" adds Gphimpy.

4   Her first few assignments include several thousand planets with established populations. Quite a few planets in Varuna's sector, however, had only some amino acids floating around in a soupy mass at the time of the last census. With great delight, Varuna discovers dozens of new sentient races!

5   The strangest interview all day happens with a planet that tells Varuna its history. At the time of the last census, ten billion years ago, this planet was just cooling from swirling gases, getting a crust, developing oceans—that sort of thing.

6   "Then life began," says the planet. "The usual story." The planet tells Varuna about huge creatures. The planet can't remember how those giant life-forms went extinct—maybe volcanic eruptions, maybe an asteroid collision.

7   Then the planet developed a life-form that was small but really smart. Unfortunately, after this species had competed and fought to take over the planet, it kept competing and fighting with itself.

8   "Oh, they destroyed their own habitat. They did a lousy job of reacting to the changes they created by heating the place up and making a lot of things that were poisonous," explains the planet.

9   At the end of the day, Varuna beams home. She thinks how lucky she is not to be that lonely planet, that single sentient being named Earth, she met today.

Name _____ **Date** _____

1 The word <u>transported</u> in the first paragraph means —

_____

_____

_____

_____

2 How often does the census happen?

_____

_____

_____

_____

3 Who are the small but smart life-forms Varuna learns about?

_____

_____

_____

_____

4 Why is it good that Varuna is a Plynchin?

_____

_____

_____

_____

Name _____ **Date** _____

5 What does the narrator compare Gphimpy's office to?

   A the capital city

   B a star-filled sky

   C a smelly methane swamp

   D a force field

6 Gphimpy tells Varuna that she "better get cracking" because —

   A there are billions of beings to count

   B he's mean

   C she's slow

   D the world is coming to an end

7 What is Varuna delighted to discover during her first few assignments?

   A amino acids floating around in a soupy mass

   B dozens of new sentient races

   C dinosaurs

   D Plynchins

8 The reader can tell that the huge creatures that went extinct were —

   A elephants

   B humans

   C Plynchins

   D dinosaurs

Unit 5 Mini-Lesson ★
Poetry

What is a poem?

A poem is an arrangement of words that uses imagery and rhythm to capture a moment in time and share a feeling or emotion. In most poems, the words are arranged in lines that may or may not rhyme and may or may not follow the standard rules of punctuation.

What is the purpose of a poem?

The purpose of a poem is to tell a story or capture a thought, image, sound, or feeling in a short and concise way.

Who invented poems?

People have shared poems for thousands of years in the form of songs, rhymes, and unrhymed lyrics. Ancient peoples around the world all used poems to tell stories. Later, in the Middle Ages, people began to think up and follow strict forms of poetic structure. Today, many songwriters and poets still use these structures to share thoughts and ideas.

How do you read a poem?

1. Read the title.
2. Read each line and try to find the rhythm of the poem.
3. Notice that some lines may contain more than one idea. Think about what each idea adds to the picture the poet is "painting." Try to visualize the images, sounds, and feelings that the poet describes.
4. Think about what the poem is about and how the rhythm and imagery make you feel.
5. Read the poem again and look deeper to find a hidden and/or double meaning.

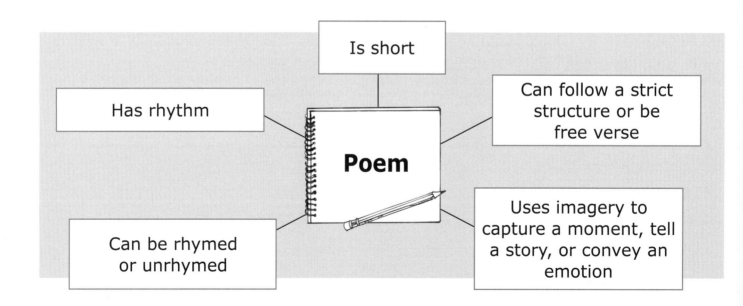

Is short

Has rhythm

Can follow a strict structure or be free verse

Poem

Can be rhymed or unrhymed

Uses imagery to capture a moment, tell a story, or convey an emotion

34

Read the selection. Then choose the best answer to each question.

At the Window

by D. H. Lawrence

The pine-trees bend to listen to the autumn wind as it mutters
Something which sets the black poplars ashake with hysterical laughter;
While slowly the house of day is closing its eastern shutters.

Further down the valley the clustered tombstones recede,
5   Winding about their dimness the mist's grey cerements, after
The street lamps in the darkness have suddenly started to bleed.

The leaves fly over the window and utter a word as they pass
To the face that leans from the darkness, intent, with two dark-filled eyes
That watch for ever earnestly from behind the window glass.

Name _____ **Date** _____

1 The mood of this poem can best be described as —

_____

_____

_____

_____

2 Describe the poetic structure of the poem.

_____

_____

_____

_____

3 List three examples of personification in this poem.

_____

_____

_____

_____

4 What is happening in this poem?

_____

_____

_____

_____

Name _____ **Date** _____

5 What is the speaker doing in this poem?

    A walking into town

    B walking in the woods

    C looking at a graveyard

    D looking out a town from his window

6 The figurative language in the poem —

    A describes the yard

    B emphasizes how spooky the graveyard is

    C brings the town outside the speaker's window to life

    D reflects on the changing of the seasons

7 The tombstones in the poem are most likely a metaphor for the —

    A houses lining the valley

    B grave markers in the graveyard

    C rocks and boulders in his garden

    D cars driving away from his house

8 The rhyming pattern of the poem can best be described as —

    A ABAB

    B AABB

    C ABA

    D ABC

Read the selection. Then choose the best answer to each question.

The Tiger

by William Blake

Tiger! Tiger! burning bright

In the forests of the night,

What immortal hand or eye

Could <u>frame</u> thy fearful symmetry?

5　In what distant deeps or skies

Burnt the fire of thine eyes?

On what wings dare he <u>aspire</u>?

What the hand, dare seize the fire?

And what shoulder, & what art,

10　Could twist the sinews of thy heart?

And when thy heart began to beat,

What dread hand? & what dread feet?

What the hammer? what the chain?

In what furnace was thy brain?

15　What the anvil? what dread grasp

Dare its deadly terrors clasp?

When the stars threw down their spears,

And water'd heaven with their tears,

Did he smile his work to see?

20　Did he who made the Lamb make thee?

Tiger! Tiger! burning bright

In the forests of the night,

What immortal hand or eye

Dare frame thy fearful symmetry?

Name _____ Date _____

1 What does the word <u>frame</u> mean in this poem?

_____

_____

_____

_____

2 The imagery in this poem describes —

_____

_____

_____

_____

3 What is the speaker of this poem marveling at?

_____

_____

_____

_____

4 What is the "fearful symmetry" of the tiger that the poet alludes to?

_____

_____

_____

_____

Name _____ **Date** _____

5 What does the poet compare the tiger to in the poem?

   A water

   B the earth

   C wind

   D fire

6 In this poem, the word <u>aspire</u> means —

   A to seek to accomplish

   B to soar or ascend

   C to design

   D to aim

7 The rhyming pattern in the poem can best be described as —

   A ABAB

   B AA

   C AABB

   D ABCD

8 In stanza 5, the speaker asks if —

   A the eyes of the tiger were made from fire in the sky

   B the heavens wept when the tiger was created

   C the stars surrendered their spears rather than fight the tiger

   D the tiger and the lamb could be made by the same immortal hand

Unit 6 Mini-Lesson ★
Drama: Play

What is a play?

A play is a story written in script form (words for actors to say and stage directions). The main goal is for the script to be performed by actors in front of an audience. Some people also enjoy reading plays in the same way they read a book, though the format is different. The events in a play are shown in short sections called scenes. The scenes may be grouped into larger sections called acts. Many plays are divided into two or three acts. Plays consist almost entirely of dialogue, or conversation between people.

What is the purpose of a play?

A play shows people in action. The main characters face a conflict or have a problem to solve. The purpose of a play is to let the audience (or readers) connect with the characters in the story and experience their emotions.

Who is the audience for a play?

The audience is anyone who likes to be entertained by watching or reading plays.

How do you read a play?

1. Pay careful attention to the dialogue. Nearly all of the information about the characters and the plot comes from what the characters say and do.
2. Note the setting—when and where the story takes place. When reading a play, you need to use your imagination to "see" the settings and actions as described by the playwright.
3. Finally, pay attention to the stage directions, which are notes to the actors, director, and designers. These are written within parentheses. As you read, you will find it helpful to picture who is talking, who is listening, who is onstage, and who is not.

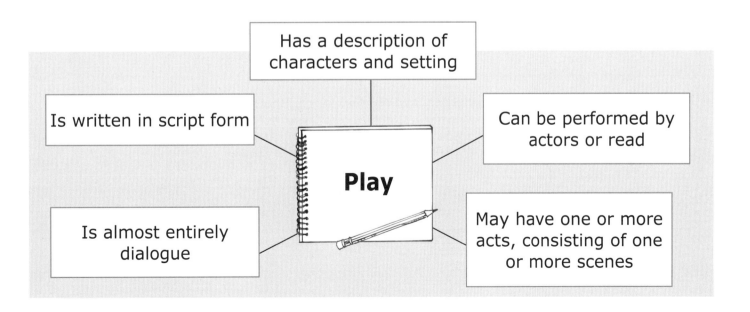

Has a description of characters and setting

Is written in script form

Can be performed by actors or read

Play

Is almost entirely dialogue

May have one or more acts, consisting of one or more scenes

Read the selection. Then choose the best answer to each question.

The Big Jump

CHARACTERS

DAVID: 16, acts tough

MIGUEL: 24, outgoing and athletic

SAM: 14, David's sensitive younger brother

Scene 1

1   (*A wooden platform high in the trees in the jungles of Costa Rica, late afternoon. The time is the present. We hear the high-pitched zipping sound of a metal trolley spinning along a metal cable. This is quickly followed by a loud yell. Lights up on SAM, DAVID, and MIGUEL, standing on a wooden platform in the rain forest canopy of Costa Rica. SAM and DAVID are anxiously staring out into the forest. They are wearing long pants, T-shirts, and shoes. They also wear helmets, leather gloves, and individual "zip line harnesses"—which wrap around their legs and chest with a hook that allows each individual to be attached to the zip line. MIGUEL is wearing a shirt that says, "Big Jump Canopy Guide." MIGUEL exudes an easygoing, confident, carefree manner.*)

2   **MIGUEL:** That was a good yell!

3   **SAM:** (*yelling into the forest*) Dad? Are you all right?!

4   **MIGUEL:** He's already on the other side of the valley. He can't hear you. But your father has a very loud yell. Pura vida! Do you know this expression? It literally translates as "pure life"—but here in Costa Rica we use it to mean "cool" or "great" or "this is living!" It's a good thing to yell as you fly through the trees.

5   **SAM:** (*yelling into the forest again*) Dad? Hey, Dad!

6   **DAVID:** Weren't you listening earlier? Miguel said he's too far away to hear us.

7   **MIGUEL:** Sí, the other side of the jungle. But now it is time for us to join him. ¿Quién es el próximo? Who goes next? ¿Señor David? Let me check your harness.

8   (*MIGUEL pulls on DAVID's harness to make sure it's tight enough. It is.*)

9   **MIGUEL:** You are good to go. A-OK. Put your helmet back on, let me connect the cable, and then you will be ready to fly.

10 **DAVID:** *(nervously)* Wait a minute, wait a minute.

11 *(DAVID peers into the distance and then over the side of the platform. He quickly steps back.)*

12 **DAVID:** How high up are we, anyway?

13 **MIGUEL:** Here? We are at twenty-five meters. About eighty feet.

14 **DAVID:** And how far across is it to the other side?

15 **MIGUEL:** Five thousand two hundred and three feet. And three inches.

16 **DAVID:** Whoa. That's like a mile.

17 **SAM:** *(to DAVID)* You scared?

18 **DAVID:** I'm not scared.

19 **SAM:** So go already.

20 **DAVID:** You go. I wish I could have stayed home instead of being forced to come to Costa Rica and pretend like I'm having fun on a vacation. I can think of about a billion other places I'd rather be. Look, this whole trip was a stupid idea. We both know why he arranged this "family vacation," Sam.

21 **SAM:** At least he's trying to show us a good time.

22 **DAVID:** No dice.

23 **SAM:** You ARE scared.

24 **DAVID:** I am not!

25 **SAM:** Why do you always have to cover up what you're really feeling?

26 **DAVID:** Why don't you mind your own business?

27 **SAM:** Why don't you jump?

28 **DAVID:** Why don't you stop being such an annoying little brother and be quiet?

29 **SAM:** Mom doesn't like it when you talk to me like that.

30 **DAVID:** Yeah, well, Mom is dead.

31 **SAM:** David! *(MIGUEL intervenes.)*

32 **MIGUEL:** ¡Mis amigos! My friends! No fighting!

33 **SAM:** He started it! *(crying)*

34 **DAVID:** You crybaby!

35 **SAM:** So? At least I'm not afraid to cry!

36 *(MIGUEL gets bottles of water from his satchel and hands one each to SAM and DAVID. A tense pause as both boys avoid looking at each other and take a drink of water.)*

37 **MIGUEL:** We need to cool off. Hydrate. One should never take a big jump when upset. That is a rule of the jungle. This is when mistakes happen and we say things we don't mean. Even the monkeys know this.

38 **DAVID:** Does anyone ever not go on the zip line once they're here? You know, like walk back down the mountain?

39 **MIGUEL:** I suppose it has happened, but with me as a guide? Never. All the people on my tour fly back down.

40 **MIGUEL:** I'm sorry about your mother. Lo siento. Muy triste. A very sad thing to learn.

41 **SAM:** Dad thought it would be good for us to have a change of scenery.

42 **MIGUEL:** Well, amigos, he picked some beautiful scenery. Look at this <u>panorama</u> *(sweeping his arm out, pointing out to the view of the jungle surrounding them)*. Here in Costa Rica, we have many, many trees and they can grow up to 100 feet tall. Your father picked a very good place to come and yell among the trees. And it can be very beneficial to yell. Especially out here in the forest, to yell and scream, to let it all out. Like the howler monkeys.

43 **DAVID:** Wait. Howler monkeys . . . that's their real name?

44 **MIGUEL:** ¡Sí! Just yesterday I heard one of them yelling—right over there. I think he was yelling at his brother. They were having a fight.

45 **SAM:** No way.

46 **MIGUEL:** Yes way. A huge fight. I'm not sure what it was about. It was hard to figure out because one monkey wouldn't howl.

47 **DAVID:** *(sarcastically)* Yeah, right.

48 **MIGUEL:** Listen, man, it's a terrible thing when a howler monkey won't howl. All that howling gets backed up, gets stuck in the lungs and the liver. Constricts the heart. Monkeys can explode from the pressure. It's a terrible thing to witness.

49 **DAVID:** You're pulling my leg.

50 **MIGUEL:** No, man. I've seen it with my own eyes. Boom!

51 **SAM:** Boom?

52 **MIGUEL:** Boom! Then monkey guts rain down on you.

53 **DAVID:** That's disgusting!

54 **MIGUEL:** You're telling me. *(He shivers.)* That's why it's so much better to hear the howling than the silence. When I was younger, my abuela—grandmother—and I would sit on the porch and listen to the sounds of the forest. She knew about the plants—all the orchids—and the hummingbirds. If my stomach was upset, she knew the kind of mint plant that would make me feel better. She was a special person. My abuela died when I was about your age—but as long as I live, her memory lives in me. If I think about her and talk about her, she is alive. I think she may be up there—on top of the mountain—still looking down at me. *(pause)* Do you understand what I'm saying to you?

55 **DAVID:** Am I supposed to cry?

56 **MIGUEL:** No, you're supposed to think . . . about what happens to monkeys when they explode.

57 **DAVID:** *(with a small laugh)* Yeah. Okay. I got it.

58 **MIGUEL:** I know it's scary up here, but sometimes you have to be brave and just take the leap.

59 **SAM:** I'll go next.

60 **DAVID:** You can't go before me.

61 **SAM:** Why not?

62 **DAVID:** Because you're my little brother and I'm older than you, all right? So I gotta go first or it will be total humiliation.

63 **MIGUEL:** David, let me check your harness then, one more time. Good. In the training, we showed you how to break if you want to slow down—remember? You do this?

64 *(MIGUEL demonstrates a side-to-side motion with his upper arms and body—like a twist.)*

65 **DAVID:** I remember. But if I'm gonna go, I want to go fast. And yell. What was that expression again? Pura vida!

66 **SAM:** *(to DAVID)* You scared?

67 **DAVID:** Yes.

68 **SAM:** You are?

69 **DAVID:** Yes, of course I'm scared! You'd have to be crazy not to be scared. But if Dad can do it, I can do it, and so can you, okay?

70 **MIGUEL:** Uno . . . dos . . . aaaaaand—

71 **MIGUEL** and **SAM:** *(yelling together)*—GO!!!

THE END

Name _____ **Date** _____

1 Why have Sam and David come to Costa Rica?

_____

_____

_____

_____

2 What clues in the play tell the reader that Miguel is a guide?

_____

_____

_____

_____

3 What phrase in paragraph 42 helps to explain to the reader what the word panorama means?

_____

_____

_____

_____

4 What does the "big jump" represent in the play?

_____

_____

_____

_____

Name _____ Date _____

5 What is David's dilemma?

    A His mother has died and he has to tell his little brother.

    B He is afraid to ride the zip line but knows the only way down is to ride it.

    C He doesn't like the food in Costa Rica and he is hungry.

    D His younger brother is scared and can't get down.

6 Which of these events helps resolve the conflict in the play?

    A Miguel forces David to jump and he cries and then he feels better.

    B Sam decides to jump first and David feels better and lets his brother go first.

    C Miguel tells the story of the howler monkeys and convinces David to go for it.

    D Dad tells David to "just do it!"

7 What is the theme of the play?

    A All creatures should respect nature.

    B Look before you leap.

    C Life is a game of chance.

    D Life goes on.

8 What will most likely happen after David rides the zip line?

    A Miguel will ride the zip line and leave Sam on the platform to think in private.

    B David will climb down the tree to the forest floor at the next platform.

    C Sam will ride the zip line and let out a big yell, like his brother and father.

    D Miguel will call their father and have the boys picked up.

Introduction to Informational Texts

What Is It?

What is informational text?

Nonfiction text is an important tool for learning. Informational text informs, or teaches, about different topics. Factual text increases our knowledge of the world.

Examples

What are some examples of informational texts?

- Textbooks
- Encyclopedia Entries
- Reference Books
- How-to Books
- Magazine Articles
- Newspaper Articles
- Online Reference Articles
- Instruction Manuals
- Science Texts
- Social Studies Texts
- Medical Journals
- Brochures/Pamphlets

Purpose

What is the purpose of informational text?

Informational text helps us learn information and explore different thoughts and issues. It also helps prepare the brain for more difficult information and for real-life reading as an adult.

Audience

Who is the audience for informational text?

Informational text serves to educate the reader on a topic. Some readers prefer reading nonfiction to fiction. They would rather get information they can use or that makes them smarter than read imagined stories.

How to Use It

How do you read an informational text?

1. Think about what you already know about the topic.
2. Think about what you would like to know.
3. Look for words you do not know.
4. After reading, ask yourself what you learned.

What are some common features of an informational text?

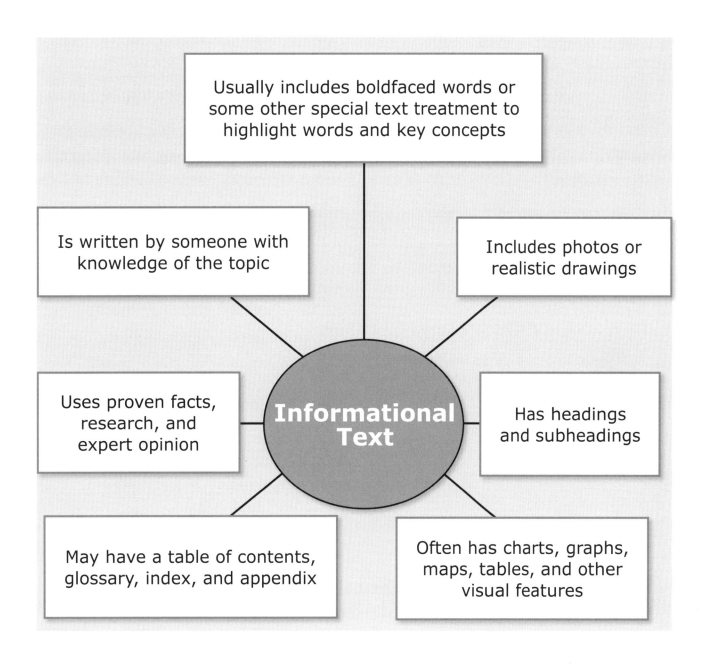

Usually includes boldfaced words or some other special text treatment to highlight words and key concepts

Is written by someone with knowledge of the topic

Includes photos or realistic drawings

Uses proven facts, research, and expert opinion

Informational Text

Has headings and subheadings

May have a table of contents, glossary, index, and appendix

Often has charts, graphs, maps, tables, and other visual features

Unit 7 Mini-Lesson ★
Social Studies Texts

Why do we study social studies?

In social studies, people learn about the people in our world and how they relate to one another. Learning these things helps give people the intellectual skills they need to be functioning members of society and to get along with a variety of people.

Why do we study government and citizenship?

We study government and citizenship to understand the organization and rules of the government under which we live. We learn how we can better regulate ourselves and participate in the process.

Why do we study geography?

The study of geography helps us understand the world we live in and its systems. We learn the similarities and differences between people in other lands, so as to better understand our own land.

Why do we study communities?

At the community level, people are concerned about safety, schools, access to health care, maintenance of community spaces, entertainment opportunities, and transportation. How people deal with these issues gives the community its unique flavor.

Why do we study communication and technology?

Communications vary across the world. Some communication is only spoken, one on one. We see people communicating through print and technology. The future of communications will bring new technologies that most of us have never even dreamed of.

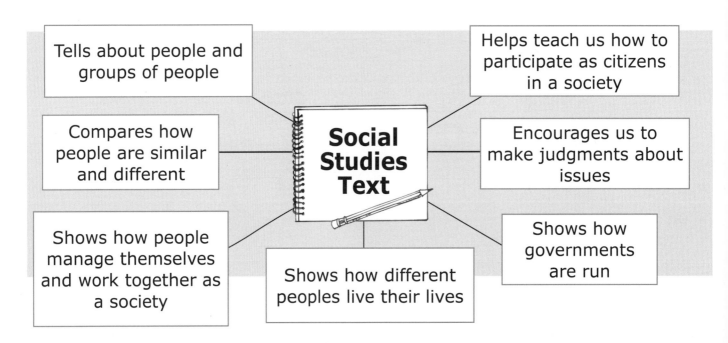

Tells about people and groups of people

Helps teach us how to participate as citizens in a society

Compares how people are similar and different

Social Studies Text

Encourages us to make judgments about issues

Shows how people manage themselves and work together as a society

Shows how different peoples live their lives

Shows how governments are run

Read the selection. Then choose the best answer to each question.

The Golden Age of Ancient Greece

1   The term <u>Golden Age</u> refers to a time when a culture or nation is at its greatest. The Golden Age in Athens occurred during the mid-400s B.C.E.

2   During the Golden Age, theater became very important. One type of play was a tragedy, in which the main character faces a dreadfully difficult decision. Tragedies were part of an annual festival that continued for many days. Prizes were awarded for the best plays and for the best acting. In Athens, there was an outdoor theater that held an audience of about 14,000 people. Greek plays are still performed today. They continue to interest modern audiences because many of the ideas and situations in plays are still considered important.

3   The study of philosophy began in the Golden Age of Greece. The word comes from two Greek words meaning "love of wisdom." One of the most important Greek philosophers was Socrates. Socrates explored a subject by asking people questions—the answers to these questions showed the weaknesses in people's ideas at the time.

4   Greek architects were also busy at work, building extravagant temples. The most famous temple, perhaps, is the Parthenon on the Acropolis in Athens. Greek sculptors created beautiful statues of gods, goddesses, and ordinary people. One such statue, the statue of Zeus at Olympia, later became one of the Seven Wonders of the Ancient World.

5   The first known Olympic Games were held in 776 B.C.E. at Olympia in western Greece. Subsequently, they were held every four years. In the first thirteen games, there was only one event—a running race of 192 meters (210 yards). Over the years, other events were added, such as wrestling, boxing, chariot racing, and horse racing. The Olympic Games were so important to the ancient Greeks that they even stopped wars for them. In 393 C.E., a Roman emperor ended the games. The modern Olympic Games began in 1896.

Name _____ **Date** _____

1 What does the term <u>Golden Age</u> mean?

_____

_____

_____

_____

2 Why are Greek plays still performed today?

_____

_____

_____

_____

3 The reader can infer that the statue of Zeus must have been very beautiful because —

_____

_____

_____

_____

4 List three things that happened during the Golden Age in Greece.

_____

_____

_____

_____

Name _____ **Date** _____

5 When was the Golden Age in Athens?

   A 1896

   B mid-400s B.C.E.

   C 393 C.E.

   D 776 B.C.E.

---

6 What was Socrates's profession?

   A actor

   B architect

   C philosopher

   D Roman emperor

---

7 The author's main purpose for writing this selection is to —

   A compare ancient Greek tragedies to modern tragedies

   B persuade readers to study philosophy

   C describe how the Olympic games began

   D inform readers about the Golden Age in Greece

---

8 The reader can tell the Olympic Games were important because —

   A there were many events

   B wars were stopped for them

   C a Roman emperor attended them

   D they were held every four years

Read the selection. Then choose the best answer to each question.

Canada

1   Canada is the largest country in North America and the second-largest country in the world. Canada borders the Atlantic Ocean in the east. The Pacific Ocean forms the country's western border. To the north, Canada borders the Arctic Ocean.

2   Eastern Canada borders the Atlantic Ocean. Nova Scotia, Prince Edward Island, and New Brunswick are called the Maritime or Atlantic provinces. They used to be part of the Appalachian Mountains. Over time, the mountainous terrain wore down, but even so, many parts are rocky and hilly. The coastline has tall cliffs, inlets, and coves. Some places also have fjords, which is a type of inlet. Inland, there are forests, farms, and swamps, which are areas of wet, spongy ground.

3   The Saint Lawrence Lowlands make up much of the southern area of central Canada. A lowland is a region of low, flat land. The Saint Lawrence River flows through parts of the lowlands.

4   The southern area of central Canada borders the shores of four Great Lakes—Lake Ontario, Lake Erie, Lake Huron, and Lake Superior—which were all formed by melting glaciers. The water from Lake Ontario flows into the Saint Lawrence River.

5   The northern part of central Canada is part of the Canadian Shield, a vast rock base made up of some of Earth's oldest rocks. The shield lies under almost half of Canada and has greatly affected the landscape of the country.

6   Western Canada includes wide-open prairies that are mostly flat but have hills in some areas. The climate in the prairies is extreme, with winters being very cold and windy, and summers being very hot.

7   Forested wilderness stretches north of the prairies. Water covers almost one-sixth of this region. The biggest lake is Lake Winnipeg, which is 266 miles (428 kilometers) long.

8   The dry, grassy plains of the prairies gradually slope up to the west and end about 2,000 feet (610 meters) above sea level. Then the Rocky Mountains rise abruptly above the plains. The Coast Range, covered in glaciers, lies still farther west. Between the two ranges are high, dry valleys.

9   Western coastal areas have Canada's wettest and mildest climate.

10   Much of far northern Canada is icy wilderness. Glaciers covered this land only 10,000 years ago. This area has the coldest temperatures and harshest landscape in Canada, making it a tundra—too cold even for trees to grow.

11   Not all areas of the north are treeless and flat. Parts of the Canadian northwest are covered by huge mountains, and birch and spruce trees fill the large valleys.

Name _____ **Date** _____

1 What is a lowland?

_____

_____

_____

_____

2 What do Nova Scotia, Prince Edward Island, and New Brunswick have in common?

_____

_____

_____

_____

3 Why don't trees grow in the tundra?

_____

_____

_____

_____

4 How does northern Canada differ from southern Canada?

_____

_____

_____

_____

Name _____ **Date** _____

---

5 Which forms the northern border of Canada?

   A Pacific Ocean

   B Arctic Ocean

   C Atlantic Ocean

   D Lake Erie

---

6 Which would the reader find on Canada's coastline?

   A coves

   B forests

   C farms

   D swamps

---

7 How are Lakes Ontario, Erie, Huron, and Superior alike?

   A The water flows into the Saint Lawrence River.

   B They make up the eastern border of Canada.

   C All were formed by melting glaciers.

   D They are in the northern part of central Canada.

---

8 Where would the reader find wide-open prairies?

   A eastern Canada

   B western Canada

   C southern Canada

   D northern Canada

Read the selection. Then choose the best answer to each question.

Economics

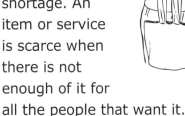

1   Economics may not seem to have much to do with your life, but it does. Economics is the study of the choices people make about how to use their <u>resources</u>.

2   Economics is also about the production and consumption, or use, of goods and services. Production is what people make, or produce, and consumption is what people buy, or consume. Every day you make economic choices when you decide what products to buy or what services to use.

3   One set of choices people make is between needs and wants. Needs are the things we must have to live, such as food and water, shelter, and clothing. Without food, water, clothing, and a roof over your head, you would not survive very long.

4   Wants are all the things we enjoy having and doing. Perhaps your skateboard is your prized possession, but you do not need your skateboard in order to survive. That is the difference between needs and wants.

5   Price plays an important role in all economic decisions. In most economies, price is affected by an important law of economics called "the law of supply and demand." Supply is the amount of an item or service that is offered. Demand is your desire to buy the item or service combined with your ability to pay for it. The law of supply and demand works like this: If there is less product than people want, the price goes up. If there is more product than people are asking for, the price goes down. An important concept in economics is scarcity, or shortage. An item or service is scarce when there is not enough of it for all the people that want it.

6   There are four basic types of economies in the world: traditional economies, command economies, market economies, and mixed economies.

7   In traditional economies, there is one system, or method of working. People in traditional economies often live in rural areas and earn their living from hunting or farming.

8   In command economies, the government owns some or all of the main industries. In the most extreme command economies, the government owns almost all property as well.

9   Market economies are the most common type of economies. All business involves an agreement between the people who make things and the people who buy things. The law of supply and demand determines the price of things and how much people get paid for working in the market.

10   Mixed economies are generally market economies with some of the features of government control that are found in command economies. The United States and Canada are considered mixed economies.

Name _____ **Date** _____

1 The word <u>resources</u> in paragraph 1 means —

_____

_____

_____

_____

2 What is the difference between production and consumption?

_____

_____

_____

_____

3 According to the law of supply and demand, what causes price to go up?

_____

_____

_____

_____

4 A mixed economy is a combination of which two economies?

_____

_____

_____

_____

Name _____ **Date** _____

5 Which is a want?

   A bicycle

   B food

   C water

   D shelter

6 Things you must have to survive are called —

   A wants

   B goods

   C needs

   D services

7 When the supply is greater than the demand, the price —

   A goes up

   B goes down

   C stays the same

   D none of the above

8 The United States and Canada have which type of economies?

   A traditional

   B market

   C command

   D mixed

Science Texts

Why do we study science?

Science helps us understand the world around us. Scientists ask questions about the world around them and look for answers to those questions, and make educated guesses, or hypotheses, about the natural world. By observing and testing these hypotheses, we gain scientific knowledge and understanding.

Why do we study life science?

Life science explores the living things of Earth and how they relate to one another. Plant and animal communities and habitats, adaptations, and life cycles are all interesting topics that are explored in life science texts.

Why do we study earth science?

Earth science is the study of Earth and space. We study earth science to understand weather and climate, as well as how landforms and bodies of water take shape. Volcanoes, earthquakes, tsunamis, mountain-building, and catastrophic storms are all exciting earth science topics.

Why do we study physical science?

Physical science is the study of matter and energy, the laws of motion, and the amazing forces that hold our universe together. Physical science texts can explain anything from the way a magnet works to the chemical reaction that allows plants to make food from sunlight!

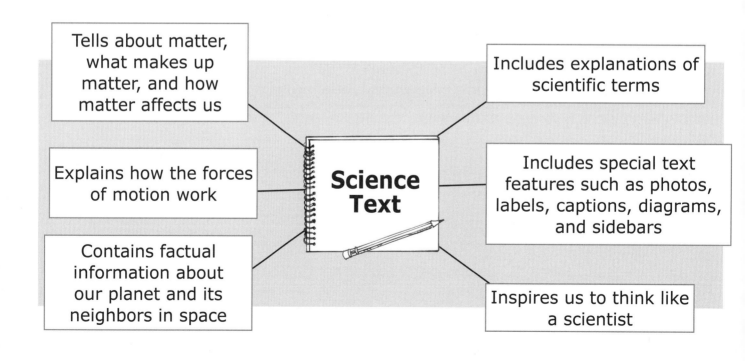

Read the selection. Then choose the best answer to each question.

Living Together

1   The saying "No man is an island" means that none of us could survive alone—we all affect one another and are interconnected. Communities of living things are also interconnected. The <u>organisms</u> in a community may help one another survive, but they also may compete with one another at the same time.

2   A milkweed plant growing along a country road interacts with many other community members. As an example, caterpillars munch on milkweed leaves. Fungi grow on the roots of the milkweed. The fungi take in juices from the roots. In turn, the roots get the water that was collected by the fungi from the soil. Members of two different species living in a close, nutritive relationship form a symbiosis. This community also includes redtop grass, whose roots and leaves need the same sunlight, water, and nutrients as the milkweed plant. The two plants limit each other's growth. The milkweed plant is both helped and hindered by its neighbors.

Mutualism

3   Mutualism is a kind of symbiosis in which the relationship helps both living things. An example of a mutual relationship involves the human intestines. The intestines are full of bacteria sharing your food. The bacteria produce wastes, one of which is vitamin K, an important vitamin for humans. In this case, the humans and bacteria are helping each other.

4   Mutualisms help living things survive or reproduce. For example, honeybees get their food from flowers. The bees collect pollen and nectar to take back to their hive. The pollen on the bees' bodies is often carried from one flower to another, which helps the flowers create seeds. Without the bees, the plants could not reproduce, and without the flowers, the bees would starve.

Parasitism

5   Living things that feed off other living things and harm them are called parasites. A parasite lives on or in the body of its host; for example, when a leech fastens onto you and sucks your blood, you are its host. People can also host parasitic worms in their intestines, fungi on their feet, and viruses in their blood. Usually, parasites do not directly kill their hosts, but weaken them, making it harder for them to survive and reproduce.

Relationship	Who is helped?
Mutualism	Both helped
Commensalism	One helped, other unharmed
Parasitism	Parasite helped, host hurt
Competition	Both hurt
Predation	Predator helped, prey killed

Name _____ **Date** _____

1 The word <u>organism</u> in paragraph 1 means —

_____

_____

_____

_____

2 How do fungi help a milkweed plant?

_____

_____

_____

_____

3 What is the difference between mutualism and parasitism?

_____

_____

_____

_____

4 What does the saying "No man is an island" have to do with communities of living things?

_____

_____

_____

_____

Name _____ **Date** _____

5 A type of relationship that helps both living things is —

    A parasitism

    B symbiosis

    C mutualism

    D nutritive

6 Redtop grass and the milkweed plant compete for —

    A sunlight

    B water

    C nutrients

    D all of the above

7 Which is the best summary of this selection?

    A Living things feed off other living things.

    B Mutualism helps living things survive or reproduce.

    C Organisms in a community help one another survive, but they also may compete with each other.

    D Some living things feed off other living things and harm them.

8 A virus in a human's blood is an example of —

    A parasitism

    B a fungus

    C mutualism

    D symbiosis

Read the selection. Then choose the best answer to each question.

Forces

1   Softball is a game of forces and motion. A force is a push or a pull that makes things move, stops things from moving, or changes their direction. Motion is any change in an object's position.

2   It takes force to throw a ball and to hit a ball; it takes force to stop a ball as well. Where do these forces—the pushes and pulls—come from? They start with those muscles in your body that are attached to bones. The muscles pull on the bones to move your body. Think of a softball pitcher, for example. The muscles in her shoulder pull on the bones in her arm, allowing her to raise her arm and pull it back. Other muscles pull on bones to swing her arm forward, letting her give the ball a big push— a pitch. The ball flies toward home plate.

3   The pitcher has used force to start the ball moving. Now it's the batter's turn to use force. She holds the bat shoulder-high, steps forward, and swings her arms across her waist; this movement is made possible by the dozens of muscles pulling on her bones. Then she hits the ball with the bat. The bat changes the direction of the ball and gives the ball a big push, using force to send the ball high into the air.

4   The ball sails through the air, but ultimately falls back down. That is because it is pulled down by the force of gravity, which is the force that pulls any two objects together—in this case, the two objects being Earth and the ball. Because Earth is so big, the pull of its gravity is strong—so no matter how high the ball is hit, it always comes back down.

5   When gravity pulls the softball down to the ground, it bounces a few times, but each bounce gets lower and lower. Then it rolls on the ground and stops.

6   Did the ball slow down and stop because it ran out of force? No, things don't run out of force, but rather, other forces act on each other—in this case, another force acted on the ball to slow it down and stop it. One of those forces is friction, which is caused when one surface rubs against another. Friction acts in a direction opposite to the motion of a moving object, making it harder for the object to move. Each time a ball bounces, it rubs against the ground a little bit and slows down. When a ball rolls, it rubs against the ground again and again, causing friction to build up and eventually causing the ball to stop rolling.

7   Meanwhile, the batter races down the first base line, rounds the bag, and heads for second. The outfielder picks up the ball and throws it to second base. The fielder throws the ball hard, but it is slowed down because of air resistance, which is friction between an object and gas particles in the air. The runner's hand reaches the base a split second before the ball. SAFE!

Name _____ **Date** _____

1 What is motion?

_____

_____

_____

_____

2 A push and a pull are both examples of —

_____

_____

_____

_____

3 How does a pitcher use force to throw a ball?

_____

_____

_____

_____

4 How does friction cause a ball to slow down and stop?

_____

_____

_____

_____

Name _____ **Date** _____

5 Both throwing and hitting a ball require —

A pushes

B pulls

C force

D luck

6 What causes a ball to fall to the ground?

A gravity

B a push

C muscles

D friction

7 A ball eventually slows down and stops because —

A of gravity

B of friction

C of motion

D it runs out of force

8 The friction between an object and gas particles in the air is —

A air resistance

B motion

C a push

D a pull

Read the selection. Then choose the best answer to each question.

What Is Energy?

1   Energy is one of the most basic properties of the universe. Light, heat, sound, and electricity are all forms of energy. Energy is the ability to do work— it moves automobiles down the street, lights street lamps, and helps trees grow and blossom. A lot of energy is used in building and maintaining a city as well.

2   Stored energy, which is called potential energy, can be found in food, firewood, and gasoline. Kinetic energy is energy of movement. It is the energy an object has because of the motion of its mass. Flowing water and blowing air have kinetic energy, and so does a cyclist riding down a hill. As the cyclist increases her speed, her kinetic energy also increases, because the faster something moves, the more kinetic energy it has. Energy can be converted from one form to another, although each time energy changes form, some of it turns into heat.

Energy Sources

3   Energy comes from a variety of sources. An energy source used to meet the needs of people is called an energy resource and can be thought of as the raw material from which energy is produced.

4   The sun is our most important source of energy. Sunlight, or solar energy, is a renewable resource that nature replaces within a short period of time. The energy contained in wind, waves, and running water also comes indirectly from solar energy.

5   Plants convert the kinetic energy of light into the potential energy of food. The food in turn provides energy for growth and reproduction. Animals gain this energy when they eat the plants.

6   People use plant and animal materials, or biomass, as sources of energy as well. Some of the energy in the remains of ancient living things is preserved deep in the ground. Coal, natural gas, and petroleum are all found in the ground; they are called nonrenewable resources because they cannot be replaced.

7   The heat inside Earth is an energy resource that does not come from the sun. An additional nonsolar energy resource is nuclear energy, which is the potential energy that is stored in atoms.

ENERGY RESOURCES	
Renewable Energy	**Nonrenewable Energy**
Solar Energy	Fossil Fuels
Hydraulic Energy	• Coal
Wind Energy	• Petroleum
Biomass Energy	• Natural Gas
Geothermal Energy	Nuclear Energy

Name _____ **Date** _____

1   In this selection, the word <u>energy</u> means —

_____

_____

_____

_____

2   How are light, heat, sound, and electricity alike?

_____

_____

_____

_____

3   What's the difference between the energy in firewood and the energy in blowing air?

_____

_____

_____

_____

4   What makes sunlight a renewable resource?

_____

_____

_____

_____

Name _____ **Date** _____

5 How are flowing water and blowing air alike?

    A both have potential energy

    B both have kinetic energy

    C both are solar energy

    D both are nuclear energy

6 What happens as a cyclist increases speed?

    A potential energy increases

    B potential energy decreases

    C kinetic energy increases

    D kinetic energy decreases

7 Which happens first?

    A Animals gain energy from plants.

    B Food provides energy for growth.

    C Plants convert the kinetic energy of light into potential energy.

    D Food provides energy for reproduction.

8 Which does not contain energy from the sun?

    A atoms

    B waves

    C running water

    D wind

Unit 9 Mini-Lesson ★
Persuasive Essays

What is a persuasive essay?

A persuasive essay is an article that tries to convince the reader of something. It is typically short and to the point. It has a title, an introduction with thesis statement, supporting paragraphs, and a conclusion. The introduction catches the reader's attention by stating the topic and different opinions. Also in the introduction, the thesis states the problem to be presented and the author's solution. The supporting paragraphs summarize the writer's opinions by giving facts and examples. The conclusion grabs the reader with strong words about what the reader should do.

What is the purpose of a persuasive essay?

An author writes a persuasive essay to hook readers into a topic and then convince them that the author's opinion is correct. The conclusion includes a "call to action." Readers must do something or believe something.

Who is the audience for a persuasive essay?

The audience for the essay depends on its purpose. Is it a letter to convince people that schools should start later? Then your audience might be people who can make that change. Is your article about the benefits of a later bedtime? Then your audience would be your parent or guardian.

How do you read a persuasive essay?

First determine what the writer wants to convince you to do or believe. Next see if the writer has made strong points in each supporting paragraph. The points should support the writer's opinion. Look for facts in the article, such as expert opinions, references, or numbers. At the conclusion, decide whether you agree with the writer.

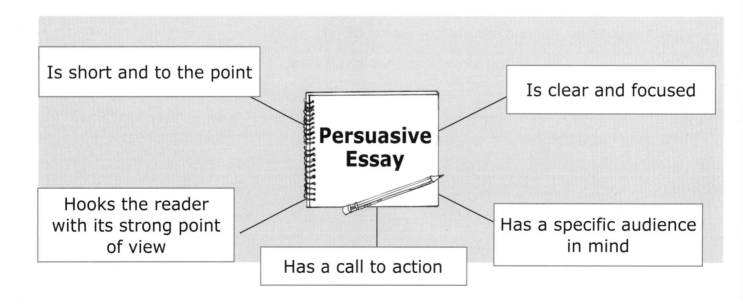

Is short and to the point

Is clear and focused

Persuasive Essay

Hooks the reader with its strong point of view

Has a call to action

Has a specific audience in mind

Read the selection. Then choose the best answer to each question.

The Best Place to Live: Cities

1   City life. The lights. The sounds. The whirling crowds of people from so many cultures and places. For a kid who wants the most out of life, a city is the only place to live. City kids can have it all— places to run around, good schools, and plenty of fun things to do. Once you've sampled city living, you'll find the thought of living anywhere else <u>unfathomable</u>. Of course, every city is a little different from all the others. Some cities, such as Los Angeles, are large and sprawling, so people generally drive from place to place. Other cities, such as New York, are built in a more concentrated area and have good public transportation (although people take taxis and drive cars, too).

2   In Boston, there's something for everyone. If you're interested in marine life, check out the aquarium, or go on a whale watch. If you're interested in art, spend the day at the Museum of Fine Arts or the Isabella Stewart Gardner Museum. And if you like music, you can go to the Boston Symphony, the Boston Pops, or try out for the Youth Symphony and make your own music! Are you a sports enthusiast? Sit in the bleachers and watch the Red Sox play at Fenway Park or watch crew racing at the head of the Charles River. Come and watch (or, if you're at least eighteen, run in) the Boston Marathon. Anyone who likes running can use the running paths along the river. Or you could ice skate on Frog Pond in winter, play soccer in any of the many parks, or sail right down the Charles.

3   Do you like great food? Eat your way through the Faneuil Hall marketplace, the North End, or Chinatown—or enjoy a picnic on the Boston Common. How about history? The Freedom Trail runs right past my school. What's the best part about all these activities? You don't need your parents to drive you, let alone come along. Where else but in a city can kids enjoy this much independence from their parents?

4   Cities have long been known as great melting pots, where people from all different places and socioeconomic backgrounds come together to live, learn, and work in a shared environment. While this way of life has certainly not been without problems, it can be one of the best things about living in a city.

Name _____ **Date** _____

1 The word <u>unfathomable</u> in paragraph 1 means —

_____

_____

_____

_____

2 List three details that support the writer's opinion about city life.

_____

_____

_____

_____

3 How does New York differ from Los Angeles?

_____

_____

_____

_____

4 What does the writer mean when he describes cities as "melting pots"?

_____

_____

_____

_____

Name _____ **Date** _____

5 Which city requires that you drive?

    A New York

    B Los Angeles

    C Boston

    D Chicago

6 If you are sitting in Fenway Park, you are in —

    A New York

    B Los Angeles

    C Boston

    D Chinatown

7 The reader can infer that the writer is a —

    A teacher

    B parent

    C taxi driver

    D kid

8 Which city does the writer live in?

    A Los Angeles

    B Boston

    C New York

    D none of the above

Read the selection. Then choose the best answer to each question.

The Best Place to Live: Suburbs

1   Living in the suburbs is way better than living in the city or out in the country. What really sets the suburbs apart from city and country living is that they were built specifically for families—so that kids could be around other kids. The suburb's family-centered design makes it the best place for a kid to grow up.

2   I live in Andover, a town that is twenty miles outside of Boston. There are just over 30,000 people here. Just like in the city, we have plenty of kid-friendly places to go, such as movies, theaters, and ethnic restaurants—but we don't have to deal with parking problems, long lines to get in, and high prices. And just like in the country, we have wide-open spaces to run around in. But the playing fields are in better shape and more available to everyone.

3   In my town, many people know their neighbors. On my street, we know what every one of our neighbors looks like. People often greet me by name. I have three friends who live close to my house. My mom and dad have a lot of friends, too. When our next-door neighbor had an operation, people in the neighborhood took turns bringing dinner over so his wife didn't have to worry about cooking.

4   Whether you're a star athlete or just like to get out there and play ball, the suburbs are where you want to live. There's also a state forest nearby with 3,000 acres of open space for fishing, hiking, biking, and horseback riding.

5   Sure, kids play sports both in the city and in the country. But in the suburbs, we have enough space, rinks, fields, and pools for everyone to use. In the city, so many people want to use the sports facilities that they're often available only to organized teams that have money for special permits.

6   In the country, there aren't enough people living in one area to make it worthwhile for a town to even build those kinds of places. So people in the country often have to drive a long way to take part in organized sports.

7   Some people say, "But what about the high cost of commuting? What about having to use a car all the time?" It's true that we have to drive to the grocery store and other stores to do errands. But the upside is that we're able to buy in bulk and not go shopping as often. It's a huge energy saver in the long run.

8   If you're a kid who likes to run around, play sports, and hang out with lots of kids your own age, the suburbs can't be beat. If you don't live in the suburbs already, try to convince your parents to move there!

Name _____ **Date** _____

1 What are the suburbs?

_____

_____

_____

_____

2 How does the writer feel about the suburbs? Give three pieces of evidence to support your response.

_____

_____

_____

_____

3 How are the playing fields in Andover different from the ones in the country?

_____

_____

_____

_____

4 What is the author's purpose in writing this selection?

_____

_____

_____

_____

Name _____ **Date** _____

5 The writer lives in —

   A the city

   B the suburbs

   C the country

   D New York

6 Like a city, Andover has —

   A long lines

   B parking problems

   C wide-open spaces

   D theaters

7 The reader can infer that to use a sports facility in a city, you need to —

   A be part of an organized sports team

   B be an exceptional athlete

   C go with your parents

   D drive a long way

8 According to the selection, which is a downside to living in the suburbs?

   A You have to buy in bulk.

   B There are no kid-friendly things to do.

   C You have to drive a long way to play sports.

   D You have to drive to do errands.

Speeches

What is a speech?

A speech is a written document that is recited, or read aloud. A speech tries to convince readers to believe or do something. A speech, like other persuasive texts, often has a strong point of view about an idea or a problem. It includes facts and examples to support an opinion, and it usually suggests a solution.

What is the purpose of a speech?

People write speeches to "sway," or change the minds of, their audience. They want their audience to see their points of view. They may want to motivate, or encourage, people to take action, too. The purpose of a political speech might be to change public opinion or persuade people to vote for something or someone. Other speeches are written to inspire, celebrate, or simply thank people.

Who is the audience for a speech?

People write speeches for all types of occasions, including political rallies, award ceremonies, weddings, funerals, and even birthday parties. People write speeches to share their views and tell the audience about something they believe in. They may write a speech to gain support for a person or a cause. They may also write a speech to convince their audience to act in favor of or against something.

How do you read (or listen to) a speech?

Keep in mind that the speaker or speechwriter wants you to support a particular position. Ask yourself: What is this person's position, or opinion? Does she support it with facts and good reasons? Do I agree with her? A good speechwriter knows her audience. She uses facts and reasons that might sway her audience in her favor. She also reads the speech aloud several times to make sure that the words are powerful and flow when spoken.

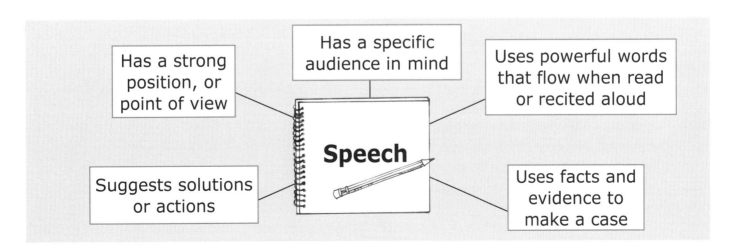

Has a strong position, or point of view

Has a specific audience in mind

Uses powerful words that flow when read or recited aloud

Suggests solutions or actions

Speech

Uses facts and evidence to make a case

Read the selection. Then choose the best answer to each question.

My Fellow Engineers!

1   We use fossil fuels every day. Coal is a fossil fuel that is used to make electricity for our alarm clocks, microwaves, computers, and more. Oil is another fossil fuel, and it is used to power cars, trucks, buses, planes, and trains. Natural gas is also a fossil fuel. We use it to warm our homes and cook our food. Fossil fuels can do all of these jobs because they are easy to control, transport, change, and burn. Other energy sources, such as solar, wind, water, and nuclear power, make only electricity and therefore are not able to power most types of transportation. There is no other energy source as useful as fossil fuels. Fossil fuels are America's best source of power.

2   Our need for energy is constant, and fossil fuels are amazingly <u>diverse</u>. They are able to do more tasks than any other source of energy. In addition, fossil fuels are by far the most affordable source of energy on the planet.

3   Some groups have criticized the use of fossil fuels. They say fossil fuels cause problems such as air pollution and climate change. They believe that renewable resources are better for the environment. The truth is that every source of energy has some environmental problem; solar cells are made with poisonous metals and wind turbines kill birds and cause noise pollution. Even hydropower dams cause problems—they drown rivers and animals that depend on the water, from endangered amphibians to fish that can no longer swim upstream to spawn, or deposit eggs.

4   Fossil fuels, however, are made to be clean and safe. Clean-coal technology takes impurities out of raw coal long before they are able to reach the power plant. Scrubbing smokestacks remove the remaining pollutants.

5   For more than 100 years, fossil fuels have been the world's most used energy source. Billions of people depend on them every day. They make energy steadily, predictably, and on demand, and their cost simply can't be beat. They make power affordable for everyone. Fossil fuels make our way of life possible. And technology makes sure fossil fuels will be environmentally sustainable for decades to come. It makes sense that we continue to use fossil fuels. They are the best source of power on the planet.

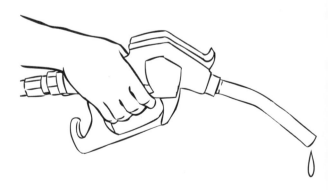

Name _____ **Date** _____

1 The word <u>diverse</u> in paragraph 2 means —

_____

_____

_____

_____

2 How are fossil fuels different from renewable energy resources?

_____

_____

_____

_____

3 What evidence supports the author's opinion that fossil fuels are the "best source of power"?

_____

_____

_____

_____

4 What problem does hydropower cause, according to the author?

_____

_____

_____

_____

Name _____ **Date** _____

5 Which fossil fuel do we use to make electricity?

  A natural gas

  B oil

  C nuclear power

  D coal

6 Critics say fossil fuels —

  A cause climate change

  B are better for the environment

  C are less affordable

  D cause noise pollution

7 According to the author, a problem with wind turbines is they —

  A pollute the air

  B cause noise pollution

  C endanger amphibians

  D cause climate change

8 The reader can infer that the author most likely uses —

  A nuclear-generated power

  B solar-generated power

  C petroleum-generated power

  D wind-generated power

Read the selection. Then choose the best answer to each question.

My Fellow Senators!

1   Imagine discovering the perfect source of electricity, a <u>miraculous</u> power source that will never run out. It can be found absolutely anywhere on the planet, so people can make electricity in their own backyards. It's called renewable energy, and there are not one but three major kinds. Solar, wind, and water power are our best sources of energy for making electricity. Each is totally limitless, widely available, and environmentally safe.

2   Most other energy resources, including fossil fuels, are nonrenewable. Once we take energy from nuclear fuel or burn coal, oil, or natural gas, those fuels are used up forever. But sun, wind, and water aren't destroyed as we use them.

3   Solar cells, flat panels that convert sunlight into electricity, can be installed anywhere the sun shines. They can turn schools, homes, and even parking lots into private power plants. Hydropower already provides one-fifth of America's electricity. The U.S. Department of Energy has found over 5,000 places where we could build new hydropower stations on local rivers. Wind power is just as convenient.

4   Fossil fuels and uranium, the fuel for nuclear power, are found only in certain parts of the world. But many of those places are outside the United States. Today we spend billions of dollars on fossil fuels, especially oil. This money supports dangerous dictators and nations. Switching to local renewable resources is a smart move for our national safety.

5   No matter how you look at it, renewable energy is the most environmentally friendly source of power, especially compared with fossil fuels and nuclear energy. Drilling and shipping oil frequently lead to spills that threaten not only wildlife, but the fishing industry as well. That industry depends on healthy seas, tourism, and other local economies. Nuclear energy creates deadly cancer-causing radioactive waste, and we have yet to find a place to store it safely. So it simply piles up at the nuclear power plants.

6   What happens when the wind stops blowing or the sun goes down? Our vast grid of electrical wires moves energy from where it's made to where it's needed at any moment. While the sun is down in the evening in New York, it still shines brightly on solar cells in California.

7   These same critics ignore hydropower as well, which runs 24 hours a day, 7 days a week, 365 days a year. In fact, the truly impractical energy source is fossil fuels. Fossil fuels and nuclear fuel are nonrenewable. On the other hand, the more renewable energy we use, the more plentiful it becomes!

Name _____ **Date** _____

1   The word <u>miraculous</u> in paragraph 1 means —

_____

_____

_____

_____

2   You can tell that the speaker is in favor of renewable energy sources
    because —

_____

_____

_____

_____

3   What is the difference between renewable and nonrenewable energy
    resources?

_____

_____

_____

_____

4   You can infer that the reason fossil fuels cost billions of dollars is
    that —

_____

_____

_____

_____

Name _____ **Date** _____

5 Which is not a renewable energy source?

   A water

   B wind

   C natural gas

   D sun

6 Which energy resource provides one-fifth of America's electricity?

   A hydropower

   B solar cells

   C wind power

   D oil

7 Which form of energy poses the least potential harm to wildlife?

   A solar

   B oil

   C nuclear

   D wind

8 The reader can tell the speaker —

   A is a senator

   B is the president

   C is critical of renewable energy resources

   D supports the use of fossil fuels

Unit 11 Mini-Lesson ★
Procedural Texts

What is a procedural text?

A procedural text tells how to make or do something. Examples include a recipe from a cookbook, the rules to a board game, travel directions, or the steps in a textbook that teach a new math skill. People use procedural texts at home, in their jobs, and in their hobbies. Other names for procedural texts are technical writing, instructions, directions, or "how-tos."

What is the purpose of a procedural text?

A procedural text describes how to do something in such a way that other people can do it easily. The author clearly explains what supplies and equipment to use and what steps to follow. Some authors include pictures or diagrams, or share tips that will help the process go smoothly.

Who is the audience for a procedural text?

People of all ages use procedural texts to learn new skills, perform science experiments, administer first aid, build, cook or bake foods, play games, create crafts, or improve their abilities in music or sports. People can find procedural texts in books, magazines, newspapers, pamphlets, instruction manuals, and online.

How do you read a procedural text?

1. Read the title. It will tell you what you can learn to make or do.
2. Next, check the list of supplies and equipment to see if you have everything you need.
3. Read through all the steps and study the pictures to make sure you understand what to do.
4. Then begin! As you work, pay special attention to any tips provided.

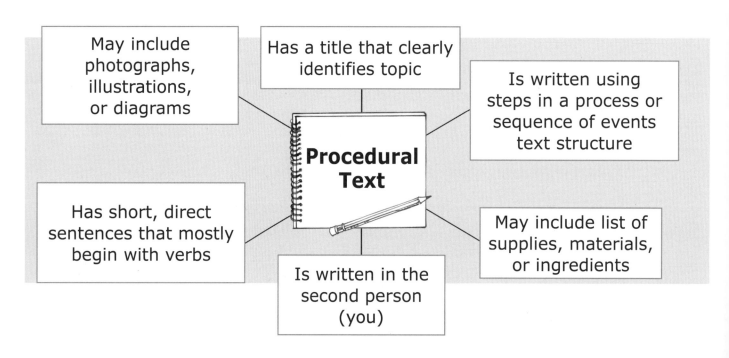

May include photographs, illustrations, or diagrams

Has a title that clearly identifies topic

Is written using steps in a process or sequence of events text structure

Procedural Text

Has short, direct sentences that mostly begin with verbs

May include list of supplies, materials, or ingredients

Is written in the second person (you)

Read the selection. Then choose the best answer to each question.

How to Set Up a Popcorn Stand

1   Do you want to make money for a worthy <u>cause</u> in your community? A popcorn stand is the perfect way to go!

2   Things You Will Need:
poster board
markers
several bags of microwave popcorn
microwave oven
large bowl
individual bags or boxes
folding table
tape

What to Do

3   Decide when and where you'll have your popcorn stand. (Get permission from the sponsoring organization or place to sell.) Ask your friends and family—including at least one adult—to help out. Use the poster board and markers to make signs advertising your popcorn stand.

4   On the day of the event, make the popcorn. Here's how:

5   1. Remove the plastic wrap from the popcorn bag, but don't open it. Unfold the packet and put it in the microwave.

6   2. Set the microwave for four minutes (or whatever the directions on the bag say) and push START.

7   3. Don't go away! Instead, listen to the popcorn pop. Remember that popping times are estimates. If several seconds of silence pass between pops, stop the microwave, or else the popcorn might burn.

8   4. Grab the popcorn bag from the microwave, but be careful—it will be HOT! Open the bag away from your face and pour the popcorn into a large bowl. Keep popping popcorn until you have all you need.

9   5. Make individual bags or boxes of popcorn.

10   6. Once your popcorn is ready to be sold, deliver it to your stand (folding table), hang the signs with the tape, and you're in business. Have fun, and good luck!

Name _____ **Date** _____

1 What is the meaning of the word <u>cause</u> in the first sentence?

_____

_____

_____

_____

2 The writer suggests a popcorn stand as way to —

_____

_____

_____

_____

3 Why is a microwave in the list of things you need for a popcorn stand?

_____

_____

_____

_____

4 Why does the writer use all uppercase letters in the word HOT?

_____

_____

_____

_____

Name _____ **Date** _____

5 The main purpose of this selection is to explain how to —

A make popcorn

B eat popcorn

C raise money for charity

D set up and run a popcorn stand

6 Which should you do first?

A Unfold the popcorn packet.

B Remove the plastic wrap from the popcorn bag.

C Grab the popcorn bag from the microwave.

D Sell the popcorn.

7 If several seconds pass between pops, it means —

A the microwave is broken

B the popcorn is burnt

C the popcorn is ready

D the bag opened

8 What should you do right before you set the time on the microwave?

A Unfold the packet and put it in the microwave.

B Make individual bags or boxes of popcorn.

C Push START on the microwave.

D Hang signs.

Read the selection. Then choose the best answer to each question.

How to Buy a Pet Fish

1   A fish is one of the most pleasant pets you can own. Depending on the species of fish you purchase, it can also be <u>affordable</u> and easy to care for. To find out about the types of fish that are low in cost and low in <u>maintenance</u>, go online, or find a pet store in your community. Then follow these steps to get started:

2   1. Before you go to the store, think about the space you have for a fish and the amount of time you want to put into caring for it.

3   2. When you are at the store, ask a worker to help you choose the most suitable fish. Then you will need to purchase a bowl or tank for the fish to live in. Get some rocks for the bottom of the tank, and ask for tips on cleaning it.

4   3. The worker will put the fish in a bag of water. Find out how long you can leave the fish in the bag before you must put it in the tank. Then ask what type of fish food to buy and how much and how often to feed your fish.

5   4. Take the fish home. Put water in the tank and put the rocks in the bottom. Release the fish into the tank. Add fish food. Enjoy watching your new finny friend explore its new home. Continue feeding your fish at the right time, and make sure the tank is always at its tidiest. Your fish will thank you!

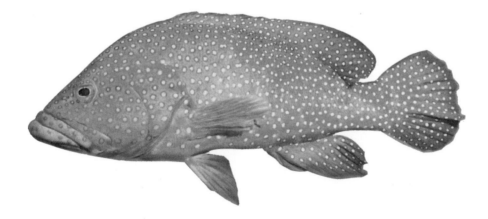

Name _____ **Date** _____

1 The word <u>maintenance</u> in paragraph 1 means —

_____

_____

_____

_____

2 Why does the writer believe fish are good pets?

_____

_____

_____

_____

3 List two ways to find out if a fish is affordable and easy to care for.

_____

_____

_____

_____

4 The author's purpose for writing this piece is —

_____

_____

_____

_____

Name _____ **Date** _____

5 The word <u>affordable</u> means —

   A easy to care for

   B suitable

   C pleasant

   D low in cost

6 What should you do before buying a fish?

   A Think about the space you have.

   B Consider how much time you want to spend caring for it.

   C Both A and B

   D None of the above

7 Right before you release the fish into the tank, you should —

   A put water in the tank and rocks on the bottom

   B get tips on how to clean the tank

   C put the fish in a bag of water

   D ask what type of fish food to buy

8 You can conclude that you take the fish home in a —

   A bowl

   B tank

   C bag

   D cup

Reading and Understanding Across Texts

How do you read across texts?

Every day we read different types of text. Sometimes we look at two texts within the same genre, like seeing how two fairy tales are alike and different. Other times we may compare and contrast two very different types of writing, like a poem and science text. The two pieces of writing may be about the same thing but have a different purpose. Or they may have the same purpose but be about very different things! Making connections between texts adds to our understanding about reading and literature as well as how we view the world.

Ask yourself these questions to help you read across texts:

What Is It?

What type of text am I reading?

- Is it a literary text or is it an informational text?
- What type, or genre, of text is it?

Purpose

What is the purpose of the text?

- What is the author trying to do with this text?

Audience

Who is the audience for the text?

- Who is reading or listening to this text?

Make Text-to-Text Connections

How are the texts alike? How are the texts different?

Literary Texts	
• Fables	• Realistic Fiction
• Tall Tales	• Mysteries & Adventure
• Fairy Tales	• Journals & Diaries
• Myths & Legends	• Biographies
• Historical Fiction	• Literary Nonfiction
• Science Fiction	• Nonfiction Personal Narratives
• Poetry	• Drama

Informational Texts	
• Science Textbooks	• Social Studies Textbooks
• Encyclopedia Entries	• History Book
• Reference Books	• Letters
• Magazine Articles	• Journals & Diaries
• Newspaper Articles	• Brochures/Pamphlets
• Online Reference Articles	• Persuasive Texts

Read the next two selections.
Then choose the best answer to each question.

Liberty's Greatest Heroes

1   America's history has many chapters—and many legendary heroes who fought bravely for freedom. Many soldiers and leaders can be celebrated, but in my opinion, some of the most noteworthy heroes were the unsung "passengers," "conductors," and "station agents" on the Underground Railroad.

2   The Underground Railroad was not a real railroad but a network of routes and safe houses used by enslaved people seeking freedom in the 1800s. The Underground Railroad was run by many people who wanted to abolish slavery and help fugitive, or runaway, slaves escape to freedom. Black and white, these women and men risked their lives and the safety of their families in the name of freedom.

3   Thousands of "passengers" or fugitive slaves risked torture and death for liberty and a better future for their children. Fugitives usually traveled by night, relying on the North Star, which is found in the <u>constellation</u>, or group of stars, known as the Little Dipper. During the day they hid in caves, woods, and swamps while they were hunted by the slave catchers' bloodhounds. The escaping slaves were on their own for weeks—sometimes months—until they reached the border of a northern state and the Underground Railroad.

4   "Conductors," "station agents," and other workers on the Underground Railroad also took huge risks. Probably 3,000 or more people secretly worked on the Underground Railroad. Very few kept written records because they did not want information to fall into the hands of the slave catchers. Conductors helped escaped slaves travel in secret, often hidden in wagons or boats. Agents housed fugitives, hiding them in attics or cellars until it was safe to move on. They gave them food, clothing, and comfort, such as hot meals and soft blankets. It was dangerous work, because angry slaveholders attacked those who harbored fugitives or had them arrested. Some were even killed.

5   Despite unjust laws, and the life-threatening penalties for breaking those laws, those who believed in freedom waded through dangerous swamps and crossed great rivers to the North to the free states and to Canada, where slavery was illegal. They did this without an army or laws to protect them. They did this in the name of freedom and equal rights for all. For this reason, I believe the fugitive slaves that sought freedom and the upstanding men and women who helped them realize their dream are the bravest, and greatest, American freedom fighters in our history. The United States outlawed slavery in 1865, but even today, some countries still have enslaved people. I hope that all Americans can remember and honor the freedom seekers of the Underground Railroad by keeping the world full of hope and working together to end slavery in other countries.

Freedom's Star   —Anonymous

As I strayed from my cot at the close of the day,
I turned my fond gaze to the sky;
I beheld all the stars as so sweetly they lay,
And but one fixed my heart or my eye.

5   Shine on, northern star, thou'rt beautiful and bright
To the slave on his journey afar;
For he speeds from his foes in the darkness of night,
Guided on by thy light, freedom's star.

On thee he depends when he threads the dark woods
10 Ere the bloodhounds have hunted him back;
Thou leadest him on over mountains and floods,
With thy beams shining full on his track.
Shine on . . .

Unwelcome to him is the bright orb of day,
15 As it glides o'er the earth and the sea;
He seeks then to hide like a wild beast of prey,
But with hope, rests his heart upon thee.
Shine on . . .

May never a cloud overshadow thy face,
20 While the slave flies before his pursuer;
Gleam steadily on to the end of his race,
Till his body and soul are secure.
Shine on . . .

Name _____ **Date** _____

1 Write a brief summary of the selection.

_____

_____

_____

_____

2 Both the poem and the selection are about —

_____

_____

_____

_____

3 One difference between the poem and the selection is —

_____

_____

_____

_____

4 In the poem, "freedom's star" can be a symbol for —

_____

_____

_____

_____

Name _____ **Date** _____

5 What words help you understand the meaning of the word <u>constellation</u>?

  A Little Dipper

  B group of stars

  C travel by night

  D North Star

6 The rhyming pattern of the poem can best be described as —

  A ABAB

  B AABB

  C ABCB

  D ABCD

7 Which word best captures the theme of the poem?

  A Persevere

  B Surrender

  C Friendship

  D Valor

8 The purpose of the selection is to —

  A explain to readers the Underground Railroad and its importance in history

  B persuade readers that the Underground Railroad was the most important chapter of American history

  C persuade readers that the bravest freedom fighters in American history were the Underground Railroad passengers and conductors

  D persuade people to keep fighting for freedom as the members of the Underground Railroad did

Name _____ **Date** _____

9 In the selection, which statement best supports the argument?

A *the most noteworthy heroes were the unsung "passengers," "conductors," and "station agents" on the Underground Railroad*

B *the escaping slaves were on their own for weeks—sometimes months*

C *They did this without an army or laws to protect them.*

D *The United States outlawed slavery in 1865, but today, some countries still have enslaved people.*

10 In line 14 of the poem, "the bright orb of day" refers to —

A the moon

B the North Star

C the sun

D the sky

11 There are few written records of the Underground Railroad because —

A most fugitive slaves could not read or write

B slave catchers and slave holders destroyed most of the written records

C conductors and agents could not read and kept few written records

D conductors and agents worked in secret and kept few written records

12 What is one difference between the selection and the poem?

A The selection is a history of the Underground Railroad, while the poem is about keeping the spirit of the movement alive.

B The selection persuades people to recognize the importance of the Underground Railroad, while the poem recognizes the symbolic importance of the North Star.

C The selection persuades people to join the Underground Railroad, while the poem encourages people not to ever give up.

D The selection is about why and how we should celebrate the Underground Railroad, while the poem is about why we should celebrate the North Star.

Name _____ **Date** _____

Grade 6
STAAR Reading
Practice Assessment 1

Reading Selection 1

Read the next two selections. Then choose the best answer to each question.

A New Life in New Amsterdam

1   "Help! Help!" the woman cried as a group of boys grabbed her belongings and disappeared into the crowded marketplace. Eight-year-old Anna watched with horror as an older boy went dashing through the crowd, the woman's purse clutched to his chest as he overturned carts and knocked peddlers down onto the ground. Anna held her basket of vegetables tightly, wishing there were something she could do.

2   Anna and her mother had come to New Amsterdam from the Netherlands a year earlier, in 1648. They had arrived on this same dock with nothing more than a single suitcase in hand. Anna's father had passed away in the old country. Anna's mother thought that coming to the New World would bring them luck.

3   "There is no such thing as luck," Anna muttered, taking one last look at the woman who now stood on the dock, crying. Anna sighed and tried to focus on her work. "Vegetables for sale," she called to a man walking past. "Cabbage, parsnips, spinach . . . "

4   The man shook his head and hurried off. Today was not a good selling day; her mother would be upset.

5   Anna and her mother lived in a boarding house with three other Dutch families. For a fee, the owner allowed Anna's mother to plant a small garden behind the wooden house. Anna's mother grew the vegetables. Anna went to the docks to sell them.

6   "Fresh vegetables!" she called again, looking around to see who might buy.

7   "Oh, Claes. Whatever will we do?" A woman's sad voice came from behind Anna. "Our journey is a sour apple. We have lost everything."

8   "Be strong, Jannetie," the man said. "We will get new belongings. We will start a bold, new life." He grinned and then added, "There is a reason they call it New Amsterdam."

9   Anna turned to see who was speaking. It was the woman who had been robbed earlier. Suddenly Anna knew that she could do something to help this couple. She said, "I am sorry about your bag. Are you hungry?"

10   The woman nodded. "But we have no money to buy food."

11   "Please take these." Anna offered two carrots and a few radishes.

12   "Oh no," the woman protested. "We have no way to pay you."

13   "They are a gift," Anna replied.

14   The woman touched a locket around her neck. "Let me give you this in exchange. It is all I have left." She took off her locket and slipped it over Anna's head.

15   "This is too valuable," Anna said.

16   "Then consider it a loan," the man said kindly. "My name is Claes Van Rosenvelt. Keep my wife Jannetie's locket safe. We shall return for it one day. When I make my fortune, I will buy the locket back from you. I promise."

17   Anna hesitated. "I will keep it for you," Anna vowed. She told the couple her name and gave them directions to the center of town.

18   That evening, Anna returned home. Her mother was outside, hunched over her vegetable garden. Mrs. Cortlandt was a servant to her plants, and they were her master.

19   "How did the vegetables sell today?" she inquired.

20   "It was a hard day," Anna admitted as she went to hand the few coins she had earned to her mother.

21   Her mother counted the coins, then looked into Anna's vegetable basket and her eyes narrowed in disappointment. "Is this all?"

22   Anna explained that she had traded some food for the locket.

23   "We must sell the locket," said Mrs. Cortlandt. "We need to pay our rent."

24   "Please, Mama," Anna explained.

25   "I promised to keep it for the kind couple. I will work even harder and sell more vegetables tomorrow."

26   Anna saw the lines around her mother's eyes soften. "All right," Mrs. Cortlandt said. "You may keep the locket for one year. If they have not returned for it by next spring, we will sell it."

27   "Thank you!" cried Anna, smiling broadly. "Mother, this locket will bring us good luck. You will see!"

28   Every day as she sold vegetables, Anna watched the men and women walk past her on the docks. She searched their faces, wondering what had happened to Jannetie and Claes. Weeks passed, and then months.

29   For Anna and her mother, good luck did not come. Their harvest suffered from a fierce winter. In the spring, Mrs. Cortlandt told Anna that it was time to sell Jannetie's locket.

30   Mrs. Cortlandt made the arrangement. After the day's work, Anna was to meet her at the trading post. Anna was sad, but knew they needed the money.

31   "Fresh vegetables!" Anna stood by the dock selling her wares as usual.

32   "How much for that lovely locket?" asked a man with a playful grin. Anna's heart skipped a beat as she stared at the couple. She almost didn't recognize them in their fine clothes. Claes looked like a dashing gentleman and Jannetie looked fair in an elegant spring frock.

33   With a spring in her step, Anna ran to the couple and threw her arms around them.

34   "It is our turn to repay your kindness," Jannetie told Anna.

35   "Where is your mother?" Claes asked.

36   They met Anna's mother at the trading post.

37   "Come with us, please," Claes told the Cortlandts.

38   Anna and her mother exchanged <u>perplexed</u> glances. They followed the Van Rosenvelts a mile north to a large farm.

39   Standing at the edge of a blossoming field, Anna took off Jannetie's locket. "This belongs to you."

40   Jannetie slipped her locket around her neck and said proudly, "And this belongs to you." She motioned toward a small house on the edge of the farm. "It is our repayment for two carrots and some radishes."

41   "But I gave you so little," said Anna.

42   "No, you gave us a great deal," Claes explained. "You gave us kindness, freely. We now give you kindness back. I have not quite made my fortune in New Amsterdam, but I am on my way! We want you to live here and work with us."

43   Anna's mother looked overwhelmed but delighted. "You see, Mama," Anna said, "I knew the locket would bring us luck."

44   "The locket didn't bring us luck, Anna. You did."

Reading Selection 2

The Law of Returns

Anonymous

Whatever you give away today
Or think or say or do
Will multiply about tenfold
And then return to you.

5 It may not come immediately
Nor from the obvious source,
But the law applies unfailingly
Through some invisible force.

If you speak about some person,
10 A word of praise or two,
Soon tons of other people
Will speak kind words to you.

Our thoughts are broadcasts of the soul,
Not secrets of the brain.
15 Kind ones bring us happiness,
<u>Petty</u> ones, untold pain.

Giving works as surely as
Reflections in a mirror.
If hate you send, hate you'll get back,
20 But loving brings love nearer.

Remember, as you start this day,
And duty crowds your mind,
That kindness comes so quickly back,
To those who first are kind!

25 Let that thought and this one
Direct you through each day . . .
The only things we ever keep
Are the things we give away!

1 The author of the story used the action scene in paragraph 1 to —

A establish the time period

B establish the time of day

C hook the reader

D describe Anna

2 Judging from the elements of the first selection, the reader can conclude that it is an example of —

A science fiction

B historical fiction

C literary nonfiction

D folktale

3 Read this sentence from paragraph 7.

> *Our journey is a sour apple.*

The author uses this sentence to —

A emphasize how all of the fruit Anna is selling has gone bad

B emphasize how sad Claes and Jannetie feel about their loss

C emphasize how disappointed and hopeless Jannetie feels about the robbery

D compare Claes and Jannetie's trip to rot

4 Anna's mother was upset in paragraph 21 because —

A Anna did not buy the right vegetables at the market.

B Anna did not buy enough vegetables at the market.

C Anna did not sell enough vegetables at the market.

D Anna gave away vegetables for a locket at the market.

5 Anna almost doesn't recognize Claes and Jannetie in paragraph 32 because —

A it has been a full year since she last saw them

B she doesn't know them very well to begin with

C she can barely see them in the crowd on the docks

D they are wearing much fancier clothes than when last they met

---

6 In paragraph 38, the word <u>perplexed</u> means —

A happy

B complicated

C excited

D confused

---

7 To repay the Cortlandts for their generosity, Jannetie and Claes —

A give them the two carrots and radishes they owed them

B finally pay them the money for the vegetables

C give them a home to live in and jobs on their farm

D pay for the vegetables with the locket

---

8 What theme do both the selection and the poem share?

A One good turn deserves another.

B Always pay your debts.

C Always look on the bright side.

D No act of kindness is ever wasted.

9 The mood of the poem is best described as —

    A chastising

    B melancholy

    C optimistic

    D antagonistic

---

10 Read these lines from stanza 4.

> *Our thoughts are broadcasts of the soul,*
>
> *Not secrets of the brain.*
>
> *Kind ones bring us happiness,*
>
> *Petty ones, untold pain.*

What does the speaker mean by this?

    A that everyone can read your thoughts, and good thoughts make others happy and bad thoughts make others sad.

    B that our thoughts affect our whole being, and kind thoughts make us happy and unkind thoughts make us sad.

    C that you cannot hide from bad thoughts, so think only good ones

    D that nice people bring us happiness, and mean people bring us pain

---

11 In stanza 4, the word <u>petty</u> means —

    A pretty

    B small-minded

    C fearful

    D destructive

12 The rhyming pattern in the poem is best described as —

   A ABAB

   B AABB

   C ABCB

   D ABBA

13 Which sentence best summarizes the message of the poem?

   A You get what you give.

   B The law of giving is a force.

   C Kindness is never wrong.

   D Stay positive.

14 One difference between the selection and the poem is that —

   A the selection uses Anna's story to teach people about being generous, while the poem offers advice directly to the reader.

   B the selection is only about the power of luck, while the poem is about the power of giving.

   C the selection is set in the past, while the poem is set in the future

   D the selection was written only to entertain people, not make them think, while the poem was written to persuade people to be kind

15 In the selection, the reader can infer that Claes Van Rosenvelt is actually a colonial ancestor of —

   A Theodore Roosevelt and Franklin D. Roosevelt

   B Cornelius Vanderbilt

   C George Washington

   D Thomas Jefferson

Reading Selection 3

Read the selection.
Then choose the best answer to each question.

Protecting Our Forests

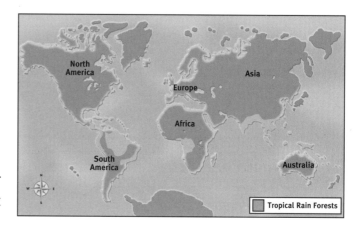

1   The buzz of a chain saw cuts through the quiet of a forest. Wood chips fly as the machine digs into the trunk of a very old tree. Suddenly, there's a loud creaking noise and a tree falls to the ground with a deafening crash. There are dozens of other fallen trees all around. What was once part of the forest is now empty land.

2   Deforestation happens when trees in an area are cut down and no new ones are planted. Deforestation is changing what land looks like all around the globe, and it's also <u>depleting</u> one of Earth's most vital resources: oxygen-generating trees! What happens to forests and why do they disappear? There are a number of reasons.

3   Nature is often behind the forces that destroy forests. For example, when there is not enough rain, forest material becomes dry and brittle. Lightning strikes or careless campers are enough to set off a blaze, creating wildfires that burn hundreds of acres of forests and take days to extinguish.

4   But forests are destroyed by living creatures as well— both animals and humans. A termite's main source of food is wood. Every year, these tiny creatures kill thousands of trees. Japanese beetles also pose a serious threat to trees. If unchecked, these pests can kill a tree by eating all its leaves and new growth. Elephants rub against tree trunks to get rid of biting insects. In time, the tree bark wears away, causing it to die because it lost its protection. But people are the biggest threat to forests.

Deforestation

5   More people on Earth means a greater demand for food, which in turn means that trees are often cut down or burned to prepare land for farming or ranching. And in many countries throughout the world, people depend on cut wood for shelter, cooking, and heating.

6   Each year, thousands of trees are felled and heavy equipment is sent in to take the wood away. The weight of the equipment causes the earth to get packed down so hard that new growth is very difficult. Is your community getting bigger? Are trees being cut down to make way for homes, new roads, or a mall? That is what deforestation looks like.

7   About 400 years ago, more than half the land we know as the United States was forest. Today, forested areas are less than one quarter of the United States.

8   Another major cause of deforestation is pollution, which is the contamination of the environment. When toxic chemicals and waste materials get into the water and the soil, living organisms die.

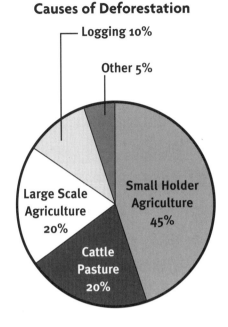

Causes of Deforestation

Logging 10%

Other 5%

Large Scale Agriculture 20%

Small Holder Agriculture 45%

Cattle Pasture 20%

Desertification

9   In some places, areas that were once home to wild animals and vegetation lie dry and empty. Over time, land that was once fertile has turned into desert. Often change in climate or drought can lead to dried-out topsoil. Wind can erode this dried soil, along with any life-bearing nutrients. The land then gives way to <u>barren</u> land. We call this loss, or reduction, in the land's capacity to provide resources desertification.

Conservation

10   How can we help stop deforestation and desertification? Conservation is one way to protect Earth's forests. Conservation is the practice of limiting and correcting human damage on the environment by setting limits on logging and clear-cutting. If people cut down all of the tropical rain forests, most of the rain forest plants and animals will die out. An important part of conservation is setting aside wildlife parks and preserves to prevent this from happening. We can take individual conservation actions. For example, many people choose to recycle paper and cardboard, which helps conserve trees. These people know that recycling reduces the environmental effects of timber mining and some of the energy needed to make new paper products. The other action we can take is to plant and protect trees in our community.

16 Read these lines from paragraph 1.

> The buzz of a chain saw cuts through the quiet of a forest. Wood chips fly as the machine digs into the trunk of a very old tree. Suddenly, there's a loud creaking noise and a tree falls to the ground with a deafening crash. There are dozens of other fallen trees all around. What was once part of the forest is now empty land.

The author uses these sentences to —

    A explain to the reader how the logging industry works

    B offer a reason for the empty lots we see everywhere

    C help the reader visualize what deforestation is like

    D persuade readers to become conservationists

---

17 What does the word <u>depleting</u> mean in paragraph 2?

    A erasing

    B draining

    C completing

    D preserving

---

18 According to the selection, the greatest threat to forests around the world today is —

    A termites

    B Japanese beetles

    C pollution

    D humans

19 Choose the answer that best completes the cause-and-effect chart.

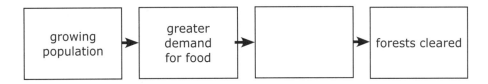

A greater demand for housing

B greater demand for farmland

C greater demand for lumber

D greater demand for fuel

20 Most forests are destroyed by —

A Deforestation, desertification, and conservation

B clear-cutting, pollution, and forest fires

C elephants, termites, and beetles

D roads, houses, and malls

21 The reader can infer that trees are most vital to human life because they are a major source of —

A food

B shelter

C fuel

D oxygen

22 From reading the selection, the reader can infer that the decline of United States' forests over the past 400 years is due to —

   A the increase in population since the European settlers

   B the growth of technology after the Industrial Revolution

   C the change in climate since the 1600s

   D the Japanese beetle invasion of the 20th century

23 What is the best summary of the article?

   A Deforestation is when people cut down trees and don't replant them. In order to slow this environmental crisis and help conserve forest resources, some people are taking action.

   B Deforestation and desertification are threatening our forests. Desertification is when land that was forest transforms into desert. In order to slow this environmental crisis, some people are taking action.

   C The increasing global population is resulting in the deforestation and desertification of Earth's forests. In order to slow this environmental crisis and help conserve forest resources, some people are taking action.

   D The decreasing global population is a direct threat to Earth's forests. The widespread deforestation and desertification is a direct threat to human life. Humans everywhere are committed to reversing the effects.

24 The word <u>barren</u> in paragraph 9 means —

   A infertile

   B dry

   C desert

   D fecund

25 The main difference between desertification and deforestation is that —

  A Desertification is the loss of the land's capacity to provide resources. Deforestation is the removal of trees to convert forest land into a nonforest use.

  B Desertification is the process of land turning into deserts. Deforestation is the process of land turning into forests.

  C Desertification is the loss of desert habitats. Deforestation is the loss of forest habitats.

  D Desertification is the loss of the land's capacity to provide resources. Deforestation is the gain of the land's capacity to provide resources.

26 The author uses subheads to —

  A show the process of deforestation

  B divide the different paragraphs

  C divide and organize the content

  D show the major threats to forests

27 The graph is included to support which idea?

  A Logging is not a significant threat to forests.

  B Farming and agriculture are the leading causes of deforestation.

  C Large-scale agriculture is a major global threat.

  D The loss of most forests in the U.S. is due to ranching.

28 In paragraph 3, the author uses an example to show how —

  A forest fires can often be prevented

  B forest fires can often be unintended

  C forest fires are inevitable

  D nature is responsible for all forest fires

Read the selection.
Then choose the best answer to each question.

The Great Popcorn Experiment

Question: How does moisture affect the popping ability of popcorn kernels?

Hypothesis: If the amount of moisture in popcorn kernels is directly related to popping ability, then overdried popcorn will not pop as well as regular popcorn.

Materials:

- 3 cups popcorn • air popcorn popper

- large bowl • measuring cup

- large baking pan • 3 paper towels

- oven mitts (*use when handling hot pans*)

Procedure:

1   1. Measure three level 1/2-cup batches of popcorn. Place each batch on a paper towel. Seal the bag of remaining popcorn. Label the towel samples A1, A2, and A3. Allow the popcorn to air-dry for 7 days. At the end of the drying period, record any differences in the appearance of the overdried and regular kernels. (You may also dry popcorn on a pan in a 93°C (200°F) oven for 90 minutes. Be sure to cool before handling.)

2   2. Design a table to record your data.

3   3. Pop the overdried corn in three batches. After each batch is popped, pour the popcorn onto a baking sheet and count the number of unpopped kernels. Record this information in the appropriate place in your data table.

4   4. Measure three <u>level</u> 1/2-cup batches from the sealed bag. These are samples B1, B2, and B3. Pop each batch of popcorn. Pour each batch of popped corn onto a baking sheet and count the number of unpopped kernels in the batch. Record this information in the appropriate place in your data table.

5   5. Add the number of Sample A unpopped kernels and divide by 3 to average the results. Record the average in your data table. Do the same for Sample B.

Data

6   The average number of unpopped kernels left after popping the dried corn was 15.

7   The average number of unpopped kernels left after popping the regular corn was 5.3.

Analysis and Conclusion

8   The experiment supports the hypothesis that overdried popcorn would not pop as well as regular popcorn. There were always more unpopped kernels in the batches of overdried popcorn. To further support the hypothesis, it would be useful to test more batches with exact kernel counts. It would also be interesting to find out if the method of popping affected the number of unpopped kernels.

Sample	Unpopped Kernels
A1	15
A2	12
A3	18
B1	5
B2	8
B3	3

Experiment Results

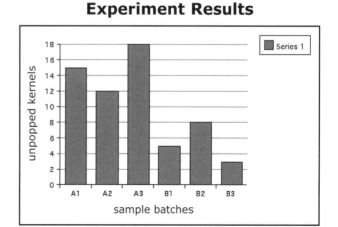

29 After labeling the towels, the next step is to —

    A pop the popcorn

    B allow the kernels to air-dry for seven days

    C design a table for your data

    D pop the overdried popcorn in three batches

30 The reader is given a list of materials —

    A to show what is needed to conduct the experiment

    B to show how simple it is to conduct the experiment

    C to show how much preparation time is needed to conduct the experiment

    D to show how you need only simple kitchen items to be a scientist

31 The word <u>level</u> in step 4 means —

    A a tool used for measuring a horizontal plane

    B to make flat

    C even, unvaried in height

    D to knock down

32 If the reader didn't follow exactly the procedure outlined in the experiment, the results would probably —

    A be exactly the same

    B vary

    C support the hypothesis

    D not support the hypothesis

33 According to step 5, if the author had 4 sample batches instead of 3, the author would average the results —

A by adding the number of unpopped kernels from all four samples and then dividing by three

B by choosing three of the samples, adding the unpopped kernels and dividing by three

C by adding the number of unpopped kernels from all four samples and then dividing by four

D by following the instructions in step 5

34 How might the author of the experiment get more conclusive results in the future?

A by testing more batches

B by not popping the corn

C by popping all of the batches at the same time

D by testing more batches with exact kernel counts

35 The next experiment the author writes will most likely involve —

A rice

B popcorn

C pretzels

D marshmallows

36 Why is it important to seal the bag of remaining popcorn?

A because you wouldn't want to spill the popcorn

B because you wouldn't want the popcorn samples to mix

C because the remaining popcorn needs to retain its moisture

D because it says to in step 1

37 Which is the best summary of the findings of the experiment?

    A The level of moisture in the kernel has no effect on the popping ability.

    B The level of dryness in the kernel has no effect on the popping ability.

    C The experiment supports the hypothesis that overdried popcorn would not pop as well as regular popcorn.

    D There were always more unpopped kernels in the batches of overdried popcorn.

38 The dominant text structure in this selection is —

    A problem and solution

    B description

    C steps in a process

    D compare and contrast

39 The author included the data table to show —

    A how to make a data table in an experiment

    B how to present results after an experiment

    C how to record results during an experiment

    D why moisture affects the popping ability of kernels

40 The author included the bar graph to show —

    A how to make a graph in an experiment

    B how to present results after an experiment

    C how to record results during an experiment

    D why moisture affects the popping ability of kernels

Reading Selection 5

Read the next selection.

Then choose the best answer to each question.

Raise the Bar: Lower the Voting Age

1 Teenagers across the United States are not having their interests represented in the government. For teenagers who work and pay taxes, this is unconstitutional. How can we solve this injustice? The United States should lower the voting age from eighteen to sixteen years old for taxpaying teens.

2 There are many reasons to support this position. Three of the strongest involve existing laws: Teenagers live under the laws made by local, state, and federal governments. Teenagers who work pay government taxes according to law. The Voting Rights Act of 1965 states that anyone who has completed the sixth grade has the skills to vote in any election.

3 Teenagers are governed by the laws of their community, state, and nation, yet they now have no consent in making those laws. This violates a basic principle of American democracy. The Constitution says that the just power of government comes from the consent of the governed. Young people should have a part in making the laws they live under.

4 Teenagers pay taxes but have no representation in the governments that impose those taxes. In recent years, teenagers have paid close to $10 billion in sales taxes per year. An estimated eighty percent of teenagers work at some point, and they pay taxes on their earnings. This is taxation without representation. Finally, the Voting Rights Act clearly states that teenagers have the skills to vote. Therefore, give teenagers aged sixteen their constitutional right. Give them suffrage!

41 Which of the following sentences supports the author's argument for lowering the voting age to sixteen?

A *The United States should lower the voting age from eighteen to sixteen years old for taxpaying teens.*

B *There are many reasons to support this position. Three of the strongest involve existing laws.*

C *Young people should have a part in making the laws they live under.*

D *Teenagers pay taxes but have no representation in the governments that impose those taxes.*

42 In this selection, which text structure does the author use?

A problem and solution

B description

C steps in a process

D compare and contrast

43 How does the author support the argument throughout the selection?

A expert opinion

B facts and details

C related examples

D persuasive writing

44 The author of the selection is most likely —

A over 18

B over 16

C a teenager

D an elderly person

45 A bumper sticker slogan supporting the argument in this selection might read —

A Democracy for everyone now!

B No teen taxation without representation!

C If you work, you can vote!

D One person, one vote!

46 What does the word <u>violates</u> mean in paragraph 3?

A disgusts

B disturbs

C disregards

D disrupts

47 What does the word <u>suffrage</u> mean in paragraph 4?

A justice

B power

C the right to suffer

D the right to vote

48 The main argument for why the voting age should be lowered to sixteen can be summarized as —

A it is unconstitutional to withhold the right to vote from any citizen who has a sixth-grade education; therefore, teenagers of any age should be able to vote

B it is unconstitutional to withhold the right to vote from any law-abiding citizen who pays taxes to the government

C it is unconstitutional to withhold the right to vote from any citizen

D it is illegal to prevent citizens from voting because of their age

Name _____ **Date** _____

Grade 6

STAAR Reading

Practice Assessment 2

Reading Selection 1

Read the selection. Then choose the best answer to each question.

Working for Peace

1   In the African country of Sudan, in a region called
Darfur, a violent conflict has killed thousands of people.
The government of Sudan wants to stop a revolt by rebel
groups. Militias attacked villages with the intent of killing or clearing out the residents.

2   Conflicts between groups of people and nations are a part of life. Fortunately, there
are people working hard to bring peace and justice to countries around the world and to
protect human rights. Human rights are basic rights such as the right to life and liberty,
freedom of thought and expression, and equality before the law.

3   Sometimes it takes just one person to bring two sides together for peace. Martti
Ahtisaari has dedicated his life to bringing peace between nations around the globe.
Ahtisaari was born in a city in Finland. His city was later taken over by the former Soviet
Union. His experience gave him a "desire to advance peace and thus help others with
similar experiences."

HUMAN RIGHTS	CIVIL RIGHTS
RIGHT TO FOOD	FREEDOM OF SPEECH
RIGHT TO WATER	RIGHT TO VOTE
RIGHT TO SHELTER	EQUAL PROTECTION UNDER THE LAW
RIGHT TO EDUCATION	FREEDOM OF RELIGION
RIGHT TO WORK	FREEDOM TO ASSEMBLE OR GATHER WITH OTHERS
CIVIL RIGHTS	

4   Ahtisaari spent fourteen years working for the United Nations to negotiate peace
in Namibia, a country in Africa. The country was ruled by neighboring South Africa.
Namibia wanted to rule itself. Finally, in 1990, thanks to the work of Ahtisaari, Namibia
became an independent nation.

5   Many groups also work to bring peace to other parts of the world. Since 1948, the
United Nations has sent peacekeepers to the world's worst war-torn regions. Today, the
U.N. has eighteen different peacekeeping operations around the world. The U.N. has
more than 100,000 peacekeepers.

6   Most U.N. peacekeepers are soldiers who help keep the peace by making sure that
all parties to a treaty fulfill their promises. U.N. peacekeepers monitor cease-fires. They
remove land mines, or buried explosives, that could harm citizens.

7   The other U.N. peacekeepers who are not soldiers perform the jobs that are
necessary to build a lasting peace. Some are lawyers and economists, while others are
doctors and aid workers. Some peacekeepers make sure that elections are safe and fair.
Others train police officers and help set up new governments. Still others help refugees
return to their homes and rebuild their lives.

1 The author includes the chart to —

    A list some human and civil rights

    B show the difference between human rights and civil rights

    C help the reader brainstorm other examples of rights

    D help further define and give examples of human rights and civil rights

2 According to the selection —

    A governments always operate with their citizens' best interests in mind

    B peacekeepers always intervene when governments violate the human rights of their citizens

    C most peacekeepers are from the Netherlands

    D most peacekeepers are soldiers

3 The word <u>refugee</u> in paragraph 7 means —

    A a person who attacks a protected area

    B a person who gives safety to victims of violence

    C a person who flees to a foreign country or power to escape persecution

    D a person who keeps the peace in a country torn by violence and persecution

4 Which country does the author use as an example of successful peacekeeping?

    A Darfur

    B Finland

    C Namibia

    D Sudan

5 Martti Ahtisaari can best be described as a —

A soldier of peace

B negotiator for peace

C peacekeeping soldier

D medical doctor

---

6 Namibia became an independent nation in 1990 after —

A a long and bloody civil war

B Ahtisaari brokered a peace agreement

C South Africa abolished apartheid

D the U.N. agreed to recognize the colors of its flag

---

7 The word cease-fire means —

A an agreement to stop fires in a war-torn region

B an agreement between enemies to stop firing weapons against each other

C a peace treaty that ends all hostilities forever

D a military order to confiscate all weapons

---

8 After reading paragraph 6, the reader can infer that —

A nations do not violate treaties

B nations do violate treaties

C nations always fulfill their promises

D treaties and cease-fires do not always include land mines

9 The map is included to show the reader —

    A the location of Africa

    B the location of Sudan and Darfur

    C the location of the refugee camps that neighbor Darfur

    D the geography of Darfur and Sudan

10 In this selection, which text structure does the author use?

    A cause and effect

    B problem and solution

    C steps in a process

    D compare and contrast

11 Martti Ahtisaari's desire to advance the peace process came from —

    A his personal experience in Darfur

    B his family's experience in South Africa

    C his personal experience as a boy in Finland

    D his family's ties to the former Soviet Union

12 Which sentence best summarizes paragraph 2?

    A Conflict is inevitable, but people are still willing to protect human rights.

    B All global conflicts will end if people everywhere protect one another's human rights.

    C Conflict does not have to be part of life if people everywhere protect one another's human rights.

    D Human rights are basic rights such as the right to life, liberty, freedom, and equality.

13 What word(s) in paragraph 6 help define land mines for the reader?

    A cease-fires

    B buried explosives

    C remove

    D harm citizens

14 What evidence from the selection supports the idea that human rights are worth protecting?

    A *Human rights are basic rights such as the right to life and liberty.*

    B *There are people working hard to bring peace and justice to countries around the world and to protect human rights.*

    C *Some peacekeepers make sure that elections are safe and fair.*

    D *Ahtisaari spent fourteen years working for the United Nations to negotiate peace.*

15 From the information included in the selection, the reader can conclude that —

    A lawyers and economists are the most effective workers for a lasting peace

    B soldiers and strategists are the most effective workers for a lasting peace

    C lawyers, economists, soldiers, and aid workers are all necessary for a lasting peace

    D a new government and infrastructure is often needed to achieve lasting peace

16 The reader can conclude that freedom to earn a living is a —

    A basic human right

    B civil right

    C the right of a citizen

    D not something the U.N. is concerned with

Reading Selection 2

Read the selection.
Then choose the best answer to each question.

Odysseus and the Cyclops

1   Odysseus had left Troy years ago with a dozen ships and many men. But rough seas threw his ships off course, and Odysseus and his fleet had to stop at islands along the way to replenish their supply of food and fresh water. They had only recently escaped from the sleepy land of the Lotus-eaters. Now, unbeknownst to them, they docked on the island of the Cyclops, a dreaded, one-eyed giant.

2   Odysseus, a brave man, chose from his crew twelve other men of <u>mettle</u> and set off to explore the island. They brought with them a jar of wine that Apollo's priest had given them; they would give it as a gift to whomever lived on the island.

3   After walking for some time, Odysseus and his men came to a giant cave surrounded by sheep. "Where is the shepherd?" asked Eurylochus, Odysseus's lieutenant.

4   "Let us go inside the cave," said Odysseus. "Perhaps we will find him there."

5   There was no shepherd inside the cave, but there were wheels of cheese as tall as the tallest soldier and buckets of milk big enough for all of the men to bathe in.

6   "This shepherd must be a giant!" said a crewman named Elpenor.

7   Suddenly, a shadow fell across the mouth of the cave. Odysseus and his men turned and saw a horrific sight: an ugly, one-eyed giant standing at the entrance to the cave, blocking their exit.

8   "Who trespasses in my home?" roared the giant. "Did you not see the gate?"

9   "We are Greek warriors," said Odysseus. "We have stopped here on our long journey home from Troy—"

10   "Silence! Do you not know that I am Polyphemus, son of Poseidon, god of the sea? Do you not know that this is my home?"

11   "If this is your home," said Odysseus, "then we are your guests. Where is your hospitality?"

12   The giant's laugh was thunder. "Hospitality? Do you expect me to have you to dinner? Ha! I will have you for dinner, and for breakfast and lunch as well." And with that, Polyphemus grabbed two of Odysseus's men and gobbled them up. "There is my hospitality," he said with a belch. Then the Cyclops brought his sheep inside his cave for the night and blocked the entrance with a giant boulder.

13   Odysseus's men trembled with fear. "We are trapped," they whispered to their leader. "The Cyclops will eat us! What shall we do?" But Odysseus was as clever as he was brave. He quickly thought of a way to prevent Polyphemus from eating any more of his men.

14   "Polyphemus, you must be thirsty after your dinner. Please drink this wine I brought for you."

15   "Wine? Give me that!" said Polyphemus. He took a giant gulp. "This is liquid joy," he said. "I must find a way to thank you for it. Tell me your name."

16   Odysseus had his answer ready. "My name," he said, "is Nobody."

17   Polyphemus gave a drowsy nod. "To thank you for your wine, Nobody, I will eat the rest of your men first. I will eat Nobody last. Now leave me be. The wine has made me sleepy."

18   As soon as Polyphemus fell asleep, Odysseus directed his men to a giant olive tree branch near the rear of the cave. "Take out your knives," he said. "We must work quickly, before the Cyclops awakens."

19   The men worked until they had sharpened one end of the branch to a fine point. Then Odysseus and his men hefted the branch and ran toward the sleeping Polyphemus. They drove the spear right into the Cyclops's eye, blinding him.

20   "Oh, my eye, my eye!" Polyphemus roared. "Brother, help me!"

21   Moments later, the ground outside the cave shook fiercely. The approaching Cyclops's footsteps were small earthquakes.

22   "His brother is coming. Now we are surely doomed," said another sailor.

23   "Hush," said Odysseus. "You will see. We will be safe in the cave."

24   A loud voice bellowed from outside the cave. "Why have you woken me, Polyphemus? Who is harming you?"

25   "Nobody is harming me!" shouted Polyphemus.

26   "Then why did you wake me?"

27   "Nobody is killing me!" Polyphemus shouted.

28   "Then why are you screaming so?"

29   "Nobody has blinded me!" Polyphemus cried.

30   Brother Cyclops kicked the boulder so hard that stones fell from the roof of the cave. "You speak foolishly, Polyphemus. If nobody is harming you, then I am going back to sleep." And Brother Cyclops stormed off.

31   Polyphemus cried out in agony. "I will get you for this, Nobody. You will never get past me alive!"

32   "Your wisdom saved us from Brother Cyclops," whispered Elpenor. "But how are we going to get out of the cave?"

33   "Do not worry," said Odysseus. "I will think of something."

34   Soon it was morning. Polyphemus moved the boulder to let his sheep go out and graze. The blinded giant stood in the entryway and carefully felt the backs of his woolly sheep as they passed through the cave's opening.

35   "Beware, Nobody! My sheep are the only beings that will leave this cave alive!"

36   Odysseus noticed that Polyphemus felt only the backs of his sheep; he never checked their bellies. He quickly directed his men to twist their hands and feet into the sheep's thick belly fleece, and ride underneath the animals to get out of the cave. His plan worked! Soon, Odysseus and his men were outside the cave.

37   The men dropped from the sheep's bellies and headed back to the ship at a quick <u>gait</u>, driving the Cyclops's flock before them.

38   The waiting crew was saddened to learn what the Cyclops had done to several of their comrades.

39   "I am sorry most of all," said Odysseus, "for they were my men. But we cannot change what has happened; we must look to the future. Let us board our ship quickly, before the Cyclops notices we are gone."

40   When they were a safe distance from shore, Odysseus stood up in the boat. "Polyphemus!" he called. "Polyphemus! We have escaped, and we have taken your sheep!"

41   The Cyclops thundered to the shore, picked up a giant boulder, and threw it toward the sound of Odysseus's voice.

42   "Take that, Nobody!" he shouted.

17 What has brought Odysseus and his men to the island of Polyphemus?

    A a giant storm

    B the need for food and fresh water

    C the promise of treasure

    D the Lotus-eaters

18 What evidence from the story supports the claim that Odysseus is clever?

    A he convinces Polyphemus that his name is Nobody

    B he cheats Polyphemus and steals his sheep

    C he knows his men fear Polyphemus and Brother Cyclops

    D he outsmarts Polyphemus twice

19 Another word for <u>mettle</u> in paragraph 2 would be —

    A mineral

    B kettle

    C strength

    D spirit

20 In order to escape the cave, Odysseus and his men —

    A put the giant to sleep with Apollo's magic potion

    B hide underneath their rowboat

    C pretend to be "Nobody"

    D hide under the bellies of the sheep

21 Read paragraph 5.

The author most likely wrote this description —

> *There was no shepherd inside the cave, but there were wheels of cheese as tall as the tallest soldier and buckets of milk big enough for all of the men to bathe in.*

   A as hyperbole

   B to help the reader visualize the island

   C to help the reader foreshadow the giant Cyclops

   D to help emphasize how hungry and thirsty the men were

22 The message of this myth is —

   A even the greatest obstacles can be maneuvered if you are strong

   B it is not the size of the giant, but the mind of the man

   C all hope is never lost at sea

   D stay the course, no matter what

23 In paragraph 37, the word <u>gait</u> means?

   A pathway

   B speed

   C way of walking

   D fence

24 Why does Brother Cyclops not understand Polyphemus's cry for help?

   A because the name "Nobody" is a pun and confuses Polyphemus's words

   B because he thinks Polyphemus is fooling around

   C because they do not speak the same language

   D because he can't hear him

IV • Grade 6 STAAR Reading • Practice Test 2

25 After Odysseus and his men escape, Polyphemus will probably —

A laugh at his foolishness

B go back to sleep

C seek revenge

D eat his brother

26 Polyphemus is a —

A warrior

B shepherd

C sailor

D general

27 Odysseus and his men dock on the island after —

A escaping the giant Cyclops

B eating their fill of cheese

C escaping the Lotus-eaters

D freeing the sheep

28 Odysseus and his men —

A are on their way to war

B are on their way home from the war in Troy

C never went to war

D will probably visit the island again soon

STAAR Reading Grade 6 • ©2012 Newmark Learning, LLC

131

Reading Selection 3

Read the next two selections.
Then choose the best answer to each question.

Units of Measurement

1   Using measurements is one of the most important ways a scientist can express data. All experiments need to be repeated to show that the results can be duplicated. Numbers and quantities are extremely important for this to happen. Imagine trying to explain the results of your experiment to someone without the language of math. Your communication would be both difficult and inaccurate. For centuries, units of measurement have allowed people to measure and calculate quantities.

2   Quantitative data tell about amounts. Numbers are used to express quantitative data. For example, we use numbers when we talk about temperature or length. Any description that doesn't use numbers is qualitative. When we describe what something looks or feels like, we are using qualitative data. Scientists use both qualitative and quantitative descriptions in their studies.

The Customary System

3   A system of measurements was established centuries ago to help people understand one another when they talked about things such as length. An inch is roughly the width of a thumb, and a foot is named after that part of the body. A cubit was the term used to describe the length of a forearm.

4   In the Roman Empire, a mile described about a thousand paces. People used these approximations to explain the distances between villages, the length of objects, and the measurements for building things. To describe weight, people compared things with the weight of wheat. For volume, they compared things with the volume of baskets, sacks, or pottery jars.

5   After a while, people realized that measurements could not be accurate if they were not standardized. Because people's thumbs can be many different widths, the length of an inch was never exactly the same. Therefore, the standard system of measurements was introduced. Once the length of an inch was standardized, a foot could be defined as 12 inches, a yard as 3 feet, and so on. Still, different cultures and countries used different standardized units. And converting feet to inches, or pounds to ounces, involved a variety of coefficients that were difficult to remember.

The Metric System

6   To avoid these problems, a new system of measurement was developed in the late 1700s. After France adopted the units in the 1800s, the metric system was soon accepted by other nations.

7   The metric system is a standardized system of measurements based on multiples of 10. Using the number ten makes it unnecessary to do conversions like dividing by 16 to convert ounces to pounds or by 12 to convert inches to feet. More important, it based its measurements on fixed standards. For example, the standard unit of length was taken from a portion of Earth's circumference and was called the meter. The units for volume and mass were derived from this length. This made the basic units related to one another. Larger and smaller multiples of these units could be obtained simply by moving the decimal point to either the right or to the left.

8   You can tell if a measurement is large or small by looking at the prefix in front of the unit. For example, a meter is a base metric unit of length. The prefix milli- means "one-thousandth." So a millimeter is one-thousandth of a meter. The prefix centi- means "one-hundredth." A centimeter is one-hundredth of a meter. On the other hand, the prefix kilo- means "one thousand." Therefore, a kilometer is one thousand meters. As scientific advancement continued, the metric system underwent some fine-tuning.

9   Soon new standards for length and mass were established. Finally in 1960, the General Conference on Weights and Measures adopted a revised system that used seven base units: the meter for length, the kilogram for mass, the second for time, the kelvin for temperature, and three others that were essential for chemists and physicists to share their research. In English, this system is called the International System of Units, abbreviated SI.

Measurement Conversion Table				
Quantity	Metric		Customary	
length		1 millimeter (mm)	0.039 inch (in)	
	10 millimeters (mm)	1 centimeter (cm)	0.39 inch (in)	0.033 foot (ft)
	100 centimeters (cm)	1 meter (m)	3.9 feet (ft)	1.094 yards (yd)
	1,000 meters (m)	1 kilometer (km)	1,093.6 yards (yd)	0.621 mile (mi)
mass	1,000 milligrams (mg)	1 gram (g)	n/a	n/a
	1,000 grams (g)	1 kilogram (kg)	n/a	n/a
weight	0.1019 kilogram (kg)	1 newton (N)	3.597 ounce (oz)	0.2248 pound (lb)
volume	1 cubic centimeter (cm³)	1 milliliter (mL)	0.0338 fluid ounce (fl oz)	0.2 teaspoon (tsp)
	1,000 milliliters (mL)	1 liter (L)	1.0566 quarts (qt)	0.264 gallon (gal)
temperature		0° Celsius (°C)	32° Fahrenheit (°F)	
time		1 second (s)	1 second (s)	

Reading Selection 4

There Is No Poetry in the Metric System

by Roberto Levy

There is no poetry in the metric system

There is no meter in the meter

There is no flavor or color or fervor

There is no loss or gain

5   There is no triumph or pain

The farmer making his paces

The hope and sweat and flesh and earth

<u>immeasurable</u>

Gone are the idiosyncrasies of men

10 Gone to the power of ten

29 The selection is mainly about —

   A qualitative measurement

   B quantitative measurement

   C the customary system

   D the metric system

30 The purpose of paragraph 2 is to —

   A describe quantitative data

   B describe qualitative data

   C explain the difference between quantitative and qualitative measurement

   D define the two types of data that all people use

31 A scientist describing the weather would —

   A use only quantitative data

   B use only qualitative data

   C use neither quantitative nor qualitative measurements

   D use both qualitative data and quantitative measurements

32 Standardized measurement began with the —

   A the customary system

   B the king's foot

   C the metric system

   D the Roman Empire

33 The major problem with the customary system was —

    A different cultures used different standardized units

    B the measurements were not always accurate

    C converting units was difficult

    D people's thumbs could be different widths, therefore, the length of an inch was never exactly the same.

34 In ancient Rome, a mile was —

    A 1,000 paces

    B 1,760 yards

    C 1,000 feet

    D 5,280 feet

35 The metric system was developed to introduce —

    A an easy system of measurement

    B a more accurate and user-friendly system of measurement

    C a bigger system of measurement

    D a system of measurement for scientists

36 The author probably included the conversion table to —

    A show the difference between metric units

    B show the difference between customary and metric units

    C show the abbreviations for all units

    D show how to convert units among systems

37 The unstated main idea of paragraph 7 is the —

A units of the metric system are related

B metric system is better for volume and length

C metric system improved upon the existing customary system in numerous ways

D use of the power of ten makes the metric system easier to use

38 Many of the units in the customary system are —

A derived from Greek prefixes for multiples of ten

B derived from human body parts

C based on the names chosen by Roman kings

D based on the names chosen by people over time

39 The names of the units in the metric system are —

A derived from Greek prefixes for multiples of ten

B derived from the names of human body parts

C based on the names chosen by Roman kings

D based on the names chosen by people over time

40 According to the table, to convert a meter to feet, the reader would —

A multiply by 0.39

B divide by 3.9

C multiply by 3.9

D divide by 39

41 The reader can tell that the poem is free verse because there is —

 A conflict

 B rhyme

 C no patterned structure

 D no prescribed line length

42 The poetic device in the poem is mainly —

 A rhythm

 B rhyme

 C repetition

 D alliteration

43 The speaker in the poem is —

 A lamenting the loss of the metric system

 B embracing the coldness of the metric system

 C belittling the value of the customary system

 D criticizing the coldness of the metric system

44 What is one way the selection and the poem differ?

 A The purpose of the poem is to make a point and express emotion. The purpose of the selection is to offer an objective history and convey factual information.

 B The purpose of the selection is to make a point and express emotion. The purpose of the poem is to offer an objective history and convey factual information.

 C The poem is not about the evolution of standardized units while the selection is.

 D The speaker in the poem is happy to write about the subject, while the speaker in the selection is indifferent to the subject matter.

45 The mood of the poem can best be described as —

   A nostalgic

   B furious

   C joyful

   D harrowing

46 Line 3 of the poem contains —

   A assonance

   B rhyme

   C repetition

   D alliteration

47 One difference between the selection and the poem is —

   A the poem is about the poetic disadvantages of the metric system, and the selection is about the advances of standardized measurement

   B the poem is not in favor of the metric system, while the selection is in favor of it

   C the poem is a description of the positive aspects of the customary system, while the selection is a description of the negative aspects of the customary system

   D they are different forms of writing, but they about the same thing

48 The use of the word <u>immeasurable</u> in line 8 is an example of a(n) —

   A hyperbole

   B simile

   C metaphor

   D oxymoron

Answer Key

Unit 1 Memoirs I

pages 7–9

1. separating people based on race

2. the Bronx, New York City

3. He was very kind and treated people right. For example, he befriended a homeless man and invited him to dinner once a week.

4. Answers will vary.

5. C   6. D

7. C   8. A

Unit 1 Memoirs II

pages 10–12

1. Cardinal Spellman High School

2. He wasn't any good at sports or games. He enjoyed reading books. He thought he wasn't interesting to girls.

3. He meets a lot of kids just like him. Nobody cares about what he isn't good at. They just like him for who he is.

4. His heart is pounding.

5. B   6. C

7. D   8. C

Unit 2 Historical Fiction I

pages 14–16

1. the opportunity to learn a craft from a master

2. a stone carver

3. She will stay while he makes her votive statue to make sure he doesn't cheat her.

4. He has become a talented carver, and he will not have to live with Lamusa.

5. A   6. B

7. D   8. A

Unit 2 Historical Fiction II

pages 17–19

1. the part of the South Tower that was hit by the plane

2. He had a fever yesterday and still has a mild fever today.

3. He sees the South Tower of the World Trade Center collapse.

4. She is relieved to have survived and to be reunited with her son.

5. B   6. D

7. C   8. B

Unit 3 Myths and Legends I

pages 21–23

1. calm and quiet

2. Nun is a nothingness; Ra is a god who created the world.

3. to bring him joy in his youth and to care for him in his old age

4. because his second eye had taken over its spot on Ra's face

5. C   6. A

7. D   8. B

Unit 3 Myths and Legends II

pages 24–26

1. the sea, storms, and earthquakes

2. He was in love with her and charmed by her.

3. They thought they were better, smarter, more honest, and more productive than other nations.

4. because the Atlanteans traveled the world to tell other nations of their superiority

5. C   6. A

7. D   8. B

Answer Key

Unit 4 Science Fiction I

pages 28–30

1. He is a pilot.
2. see-through
3. He thought he was having a nightmare.
4. near the halfway point between Earth and the faraway star of Tau Ceti
5. B   6. C
7. A   8. D

Unit 4 Science Fiction II

pages 31–33

1. carried from one place to another
2. every ten billion years
3. human beings on Earth
4. She carries her own ecosystem and has extra defenses against outside forces that might disrupt her breathing and nourishment.
5. C   6. A
7. B   8. D

Unit 5 Poetry I

pages 35–37

1. Answers may vary, but suggested answers may include: serious, thoughtful, pensive, reflective
2. 3 stanzas each consisting of three long lines that have an ABA rhyming pattern
3. Answers may vary, but can include any of the three: pine-tree bending to listen; autumn wind muttering, poplars hysterically laughing, house closing its own shutters, light of the streetlamps starting to bleed; leaves flying and uttering
4. The speaker is standing at his window at the end of the day observing the limited view and the action therein.
5. D   6. C
7. A   8. C

Unit 5 Poetry II

pages 38–40

1. make or design
2. a tiger in the jungle, and the speaker imagines how the tiger was created
3. The speaker is marveling at what or who could have thought up and made a creature as mighty and majestic and full of fire as the tiger.
4. the balance of stripes on the face of the tiger
5. D   6. B
7. C   8. D

Answer Key

Unit 6 Drama: Play

pages 42–47

1. on vacation with their father after the death of their mother

2. his T-shirt says "Guide" in the stage directions; he is continually checking their harnesses on the zip line; he is from Costa Rica and knows a lot about the jungle

3. "sweeping his arm out, pointing out to the view of the jungle surrounding them"

4. Answers may vary, but may include: overcoming fear, moving forward, embracing life

5. B   6. C
7. D   8. C

Unit 7 Social Studies I

pages 51–53

1. a time when a culture or nation is at its greatest

2. The ideas found in them are still considered important.

3. It later became one of the Seven Wonders of the Ancient World.

4. Plays were performed in a theater that seated 14,000 people; the study of philosophy began; the Parthenon was built.

5. B   6. C
7. D   8. B

Unit 7 Social Studies II

pages 54–56

1. a region of low, flat land

2. They are the Maritime provinces.

3. It is too cold.

4. Northern Canada has colder temperatures and harsher landscape.

5. B   6. A
7. C   8. B

Unit 7 Social Studies III

pages 57–59

1. things that are valuable or useful to people

2. Production means making something, whereas consumption means buying it.

3. shortage of supply

4. market and command

5. A   6. C
7. B   8. D

Unit 8 Science I

pages 61–63

1. a living thing

2. The roots of a milkweed plant get water from the fungi.

3. Mutualism helps both living things survive and reproduce. Parasitism weakens the host, making it more difficult for the host to survive and reproduce.

4. All living things are interconnected.

5. C   6. D
7. C   8. A

Answer Key

Unit 8 Science II

pages 64–66

1. any change in an object's position
2. force
3. The muscles in a pitcher's shoulder pull on the bones of her arm. This pulling raises her arm back. Other muscles pull on bones to swing her arm forward.
4. When the ball bounces, it rubs against the ground, causing friction to build. Friction acts in the opposite direction of the ball, making it more difficult for the ball to move.

5. C   6. A
7. B   8. A

Unit 8 Science III

pages 67–69

1. the ability to do work
2. They are all forms of energy.
3. Firewood has potential energy, whereas blowing air has kinetic energy.
4. Nature replaces it in a short time.

5. B   6. C
7. C   8. A

Unit 9 Persuasive Essays I

pages 71–73

1. something that cannot even be imagined
2. Answers will vary.
3. Los Angeles is large and sprawling. New York City is more concentrated and has good public transportation.
4. areas where people from different places and with different backgrounds live near each other in a shared environment

5. B   6. C
7. D   8. B

Unit 9 Persuasive Essays II

pages 74–76

1. an area for living just outside of a city
2. The author thinks suburbs are a great place for a kid to grow up; responses will vary.
3. Because people live closer together, the playing fields are nearby, and there are enough people to play organized sports with.
4. to convince readers that suburbs are the best place to live, especially for kids

5. B   6. D
7. A   8. D

Unit 10 Speeches I

pages 78–80

1. capable of doing many things
2. Answers will vary.
3. Fossil fuels make energy steadily, predictably, and on demand, and their cost can't be beat.
4. It drowns rivers and animals that depend on the water.

5. D   6. A
7. B   8. C

Unit 10 Speeches II

pages 81–83

1. capable of doing remarkable things
2. He calls them "our best sources of energy for making electricity."
3. The supply of renewable energy is unlimited. The supply of nonrenewable energy is limited and is constantly shrinking.
4. They are scarce and often must be acquired from other nations.

5. C   6. A
7. A   8. A

Answer Key

Unit 11 Procedural Texts I

pages 85–87

1. something to be supported, such as a charity, team, or other organization
2. make money for a worthy cause
3. You will need it to pop the popcorn.
4. to make sure readers pay attention to the warning
5. D   6. B
7. C   8. A

Unit 11 Procedural Texts II

pages 88–90

1. care and feeding
2. They are pleasant, affordable, and easy to care for.
3. Go online, or find a pet store in your community.
4. to convince readers to consider having fish as pets
5. D   6. C
7. A   8. C

Reading and Understanding Across Texts

pages 92–96

1. Answers may vary.
2. fugitive slaves escaping to freedom
3. Answers may vary.
4. Answers may vary; suggested answers may include: hope, The Underground Railroad.
5. B   6. A   7. A   8. C
9. C   10. C   11. D   12. B

STAAR Practice Test 1

pages 97–119

1. C   2. B   3. C   4. C
5. D   6. D   7. C   8. D
9. C   10. B   11. B   12. C
13. A   14. A   15. A   16. C
17. B   18. D   19. B   20. B
21. D   22. A   23. C   24. A
25. A   26. C   27. B   28. B
29. B   30. A   31. C   32. B
33. C   34. D   35. B   36. C
37. C   38. C   39. C   40. B
41. D   42. A   43. B   44. C
45. B   46. C   47. D   48. B

STAAR Practice Test 2

pages 120–139

1. D   2. D   3. C   4. C
5. B   6. B   7. B   8. B
9. B   10. B   11. C   12. A
13. B   14. B   15. C   16. A
17. B   18. D   19. D   20. D
21. C   22. B   23. C   24. A
25. C   26. B   27. C   28. B
29. B   30. C   31. D   32. A
33. C   34. A   35. B   36. B
37. D   38. B   39. A   40. C
41. C   42. C   43. D   44. A
45. A   46. A   47. A   48. D

STAAR Reading Grade 6 • ©2012 Newmark Learning, LLC